SUPPLY TEACHING:

THE ESSENTIAL GUIDE

written by

Heather Reid B.Ed, DipM

published by

Resources Plus Ltd

Copyright © 2006 Resources Plus Ltd

Published by Resources Plus Ltd

Copies available from:

Resources Plus Limited
Unit 22b
Fareham Enterprise Centre
Hackett Way
Fareham
Hampshire
PO14 1TH

Tel: 01329 825550

Email: info@resourcesplus.co.uk

Website: www.resourcesplus.co.uk

A catalogue record for this book is available from the British Library.

ISBN 0-9552947-0-3

ISBN 978-0-9552947-0-9

Typeset by Resources Plus, Fareham, Hampshire
Printed by Blackmore Ltd, 01747 853034

Contents

Acknowledgements

I would like to thank the following:

Paul Robinson, for his support, advice and expertise

Mary Robinson, for her encouragement and support

Emma Bennet, Oasis (part of the Staffwise Group), for her time and expert advice

Gavin Thomas, for the cover design (www.gtdc.co.uk)

I would also like to thank the following for suggesting activities and checking copy:

Janet Robinson, Totternhoe Lower School; Jane Wood, Hayeswood First School; John Beck, Nikki Burnham, Roger Hutchin, Andy Ledward, and the Maths team at Brookfield Community School and Language College.

Introduction

I have written *Supply Teaching: The Essential Guide* in the hope that it will help supply teachers, schools, school cover co-ordinators, cover supervisors, local education authorities (LEAs) and supply agencies to work together to ensure that their supply experience is one that benefits everyone concerned, especially the pupils.

The *Guide* draws on my own experiences as a supply teacher, along with the experiences of friends and colleagues that I have met along the way. Some of the advice will seem like common sense, and it is. But it seems that sometimes the obvious needs to be pointed out just to remind us, or to reassure us, that we are on the right track.

I must confess that I enjoy being a supply teacher. It can be challenging, but it can also be rewarding.

I have been lucky enough to cover lessons at some very supportive schools. That is not to say that some have not been difficult. And I am not saying I enjoyed every class – but then I do not think many teachers on permanent contracts could say that either.

Supply teachers provide a valuable service. Without them, a school would either have to ask school staff to cover all the lessons where teachers are absent, or send the pupils home. And we need supply agencies to match schools and teachers to each other.

Despite this, it seems that there are all too many tales of woe. Teachers complain about the lack of contact from their agencies, or say how the lack of support from their schools has compromised their ability to do their job; schools complain about unprofessional or unco-operative supply teachers; and agencies complain about lack of information from schools and teachers.

I have tried to avoid writing a guide that implies that everything could be perfect, or that I have all the answers. We all get times when we wonder what would have happened if we had tried a different approach. We just have to accept that there are some situations and some classes where nothing would have got the result we wanted. This is not the end of the world – and we are not alone.

I hope the *Guide* will help everyone involved: the schools, the staff, the supply teachers, the supply agencies, the local education authorities and the pupils.

Heather Reid

THE SUPPLY TEACHER

People Who Become Supply Teachers

People become supply teachers for a variety of reasons. This seems largely to depend on their personal life and the point they have reached in their professional career.

Homemakers

Traditionally, many supply teachers have been parents or homemakers wanting to continue their career but with the added flexibility that supply teaching can bring.

As a supply teacher you can choose to take short-term contracts that do not involve long hours of preparation or marking, and do not require attendance at after-school meetings or parents' evenings. This means this time is free for you to spend with your family.

You can also decide on a day-to-day basis whether or not you are going to work so, when your children are ill, you can choose not to work on those days without worrying about letting your colleagues down or having to set cover work.

Anti-bureaucrats

For some teachers the balance in their jobs feels wrong. They may have been teaching for many years, and now seem to spend more time dealing with bureaucracy and its associated paperwork than actually teaching.

One way to redress this balance is to become a supply teacher taking short-term contracts. This will significantly reduce the amount of paperwork you are involved in, and will cut down on the amount of reports and profiles that you have to write, meetings you have to attend and the amount of preparation and marking you have to do.

Newly Qualified Teachers (NQTs)

A growing proportion of supply teachers are newly qualified teachers (NQTs).

For some NQTs the promised wealth of job opportunities has failed to materialise and the only way into teaching is via the supply-teacher route. Some may want to see behind the scenes of schools they are interested in before making a long-term commitment. For others it is a way of building up a broad range of experience in a fairly short space of time.

If you are an NQT, however, you should bear in mind that you can only do four terms of supply work before having to start your induction year. After this time you will be barred from doing supply, unless you apply for and are granted an extension period *(see page 38 for more details)*.

Returners

People who trained as teachers but have left the profession can use the supply-teacher route as a way of returning to teaching.

It is a good way of testing the water, as you can try out different schools and increase the number of days you are available to work each week as and when you feel ready.

Masochists

I strongly believe there must be an element of this in all of us!

Pros and Cons of Being a Supply Teacher

Pros

- You can choose when you are available to work.

- The daily pay rate can be better than on a permanent contract.

- If you get a long-term supply contract, you can get all the job satisfaction of building up teacher-pupil relationships just as you would with a permanent contract.

- It is an ideal way of experimenting with different approaches in different schools.

- You get plenty of variety: different schools, subjects and classes.

- A good agency will do what it can to help you feel part of a team.

- If you enjoy thinking on your feet, it can be stimulating.

- You learn a lot about subjects outside your specialism.

- You learn a lot about classroom management.

- If you do not like a school you do not have to go back.

- You do not have to attend after-school meetings on short-term supply contracts.

- You do not have to take marking home, or do end-of-term reports, if you are on a short-term contract.

- You can get to know a school before committing to a long-term contract.

Cons

- Just because you want to work on a particular day, it does not mean you will get a booking.

- It is difficult to plan if you do not know whether or not you are going to get work.

- It is difficult to budget if you do not know if you have got work coming in or not.

- Every day at a new school is like a first day.

- You cannot guarantee that cover work will have been set for you.

- You may only get up to a maximum of four weeks paid holiday in a year.

- You do not always get to see the pupils' progress.

- You may miss the feeling of being part of a team.

- It can be lonely.

- Some pupils will test supply teachers and try to make life difficult for you.

- Some teachers will treat you like a second-class citizen (if you are lucky!).

- You do not know what is going to hit you until it does (hopefully not literally!).

What You Need to Become a Supply Teacher

In order to be considered as a supply teacher, you must have:

- gained Qualified Teacher Status (QTS). This is usually achieved on gaining an appropriate teaching qualification such as a Bachelor of Education (B.Ed) or Postgraduate Certificate of Education (PGCE), or by following an appropriate programme offered by the Training and Development Agency (TDA).

- successfully completed your induction period (if qualified after May 1999)

- a valid enhanced disclosure certificate from the Criminal Records Bureau (CRB) (*see* page 11)

- satisfactory references

- registered with the General Teaching Council (GTC)

- the legal right to work in the UK.

Although not compulsory, the following are also helpful:

- a sense of humour

- some common sense

- a thick skin

- the ability to think on your feet

- a sense of direction (so you can reach the exit as quickly as possible!).

If you are not British, or if you qualified abroad, *see* pages 40 and 41 for further details on how to become a supply teacher.

How to Find Work

The amount of work available for supply teachers varies between counties, subjects and stages of education.

Whatever the situation, you can guarantee that you will not find any work at all unless you make sure the schools know that you are available, what you teach, and how to reach you.

There are essentially three ways to do this. You can contact:

- individual schools

- local education authorities (LEAs)

- employment or supply agencies.

Everyone has their own tales to tell about the success of one approach over another, and there is nothing to stop you using a combination of two or even all three options.

To some extent the approach that you decide to take will depend on where you live and your own particular situation and preferences.

Whichever option you choose, your performance once you are in a school will obviously affect how much work you will be offered by that school in the future.

Most schools are on tight budgets and this will affect their decisions regarding cover for staff absences. If you are the type of supply teacher who goes into schools expecting to do little more than babysit a class, then do not complain when your job disappears because the school is using cover supervisors. However, if you are a supply teacher who goes into school expecting to teach, to manage class behaviour and to provide a professional service, then it is more likely that your efforts will be appreciated and rewarded with repeat bookings.

In the following pages, each option is briefly described, along with the pros and cons of each one.

Individual Schools

Working with individual schools is the most direct route, as it means that you do not have to work through a third party such as a local education authority (LEA) or supply agency.

It may be that you prefer to find work for yourself by contacting schools personally, although some people find this approach difficult.

You are obviously free to contact as many schools as you wish, and in whichever way you feel most comfortable with, for example by letter, telephone or email.

The advantages of this approach are that you only need to contact the schools that you are interested in working for, the school does not have to pay an additional fee over and above your salary to an agency, and you can build up a relationship with the schools that give you work.

The disadvantages are that you will probably have to contact quite a large number of schools before gaining work, it can be difficult to reach the person you need to speak to, you will have to be interviewed by every school that is interested, and you will be responsible for maintaining contact with the individual schools if you do not have regular work from them. This can involve quite a lot of repetitive work.

If you choose this route, you should remember that if you become dependent on one school, you could find yourself in a difficult situation if it suddenly decides that it does not need your services any more.

Local Education Authorities (LEAs)

If your LEA operates a supply pool, then this may be the route for you.

Essentially, the LEA will add your name to a list of approved supply teachers that is made available to head teachers in the county, usually via a secure internet site.

The approach and level of involvement of LEAs in supply teaching varies significantly between counties. Some LEAs seem to have no involvement at all, others are highly active. Terms and conditions also vary between LEAs.

The advantages of going into supply teaching via an LEA are that in some authorities this is the preferred route among schools, you usually only have to complete one application form and attend one interview (although some schools will also want to interview you themselves), and you have the opportunity to contribute to the Teachers' Pension Scheme. An additional benefit for teachers on long-term contracts is that you may be paid over the holidays if you have worked at the same school for a whole term.

If you are at the top of your scale you will probably get paid a better rate than through an agency. The LEA will calculate your salary in accordance with your position on the teachers' pay spine, and as long as you work during 26 weeks of the possible 39 weeks in a school year, your LEA should move you up the pay scale in the same way as if you were on a permanent contract. Your salary is usually paid on a monthly basis and is paid after tax.

The disadvantages are that not all LEAs get involved in working with supply teachers, and those that do often do little more than set up a register. Very few appear to be proactive in finding work for teachers on their lists. The process of getting on to the register can also be a lengthy one. A further disadvantage is that you do not usually get holiday pay if working on short-term contracts.

LEAs that provide schools in England with supply teachers are eligible to apply for the Quality Mark, which was launched in 2002 as a joint initiative between the Department for Education and Skills (DfES) and the Recruitment and Employment Confederation (REC). The Quality Mark sets minimum standards for the recruitment and interviewing of supply teachers, and the monitoring and management of their performance.

Employment Agencies and Supply Agencies

Many people prefer to find work through employment agencies which, when dealing with education, are generally known as supply agencies.

At the time of writing, *The Times Educational Supplement* regularly carried three or four pages of adverts from supply agencies trying to attract more teachers to sign up. Some operate nationally, with branches around the country, others are small-scale local businesses. (*See* advertisements at the front of this section and page 142 for details of supply agencies.)

Some agencies pay according to the teachers' pay spine, others have set rates that relate to the work being undertaken for the supply agency (e.g. long- or short-term contracts). They all appear to offer comparable terms and conditions.

Whatever their method of calculating pay, be aware that agencies are not allowed to charge their workers for finding them work (*see* Employment Agency Act 1973).

Supply agencies usually pay on a weekly basis, one week in arrears. They are responsible for deducting National Insurance (NI) and Pay As You Earn (PAYE). Agencies should pay up to four weeks annual holiday pay (as laid out in the EU Working Time Directive 2003).

The advantages of working through a supply agency are that as a commercial organisation it is in its interests to place as many teachers in work as it can. Therefore it should be proactive in finding you work. It should be ringing schools to tell them about you, and sending your details to any schools that it thinks might be interested in you.

You also only have to complete one application form and attend one interview per agency. Your agency should be responsible for ensuring your CRB disclosure is up to date and will usually pay the associated fee.

If you are lucky enough to sign up with a good agency, you will also, hopefully, benefit from its efforts to make you feel part of the team.

A further advantage of working through an agency is that it may also be able to find you temporary work during the school holidays, for example in an administrative post, if you are looking for work at that time.

The disadvantages are that as a commercial organisation the agency needs to make a profit, and will therefore add its percentage on to the teacher's salary in the charge to the school. As a result, some schools prefer the cheaper options of working directly with teachers or through local education authorities (LEAs). There also appears to be quite a difference in the quality of service provided by agencies.

A further disadvantage, which will only apply if you are hoping to be offered a permanent contract with a school, is that some agencies will charge the school a fee, essentially to 'compensate' it for lost earnings. This can be several thousand pounds and could affect a school's decision as to whether it can afford to employ you.

Choosing Your Agency

There are so many supply agencies to choose from, it can be difficult to know where to start. Every week, you will find pages of them advertising in *The Times Educational Supplement*. You will probably also find a few advertising in your local paper and listed in your local telephone directory. There is also a page of advertisements at the front of this section and a list of agencies, with contact details, on page 142.

Choosing the right agency for you will depend on a number of factors. I have listed below some questions you may find it useful to ask. In some cases you may be able to find the answer by asking the agency, in others you may be better asking other supply teachers. It is always useful if you know someone who is already with an agency. You cannot guarantee that you will have the same kind of experience, but at least it will give you an idea.

- Is it a small or a large agency? How does this affect its service to its supply teachers?

- How much does the agency pay? Is this negotiable?

- How efficient is the agency?

- How much work will they find you?

- Do they pay on time?

- How honest are they in their descriptions of schools?

- What makes this agency different or better than the rest?

Bear in mind that the agency that pays its teachers the highest rate may not be the same one that is able to offer the most work. It is up to you to decide whether you would prefer three days work at £100 per day, or two days work at £125 per day.

I have been lucky enough to be with two agencies that I have been very happy with. What worked for me may not work for you, but I started by looking through the advertisements in *The TES* and local newspapers. I then rang quite a lot of agencies and asked for details and application forms. I read through their paperwork and rang back to ask questions that I did not feel were answered in the information I had been sent.

Both the agencies I signed with were relatively small but growing businesses, both offered competitive rates of pay and in each case I felt that the consultant who interviewed me treated me like an individual rather than a commodity who was going to earn them commission. In the end, I suppose my choice was down to a gut feeling.

You might also find it useful to find out whether the agencies are members of the Recruitment and Employment Confederation (REC), the self-regulatory body for the employment agency industry (*see* page 143), and if they have the Quality Mark, which is awarded by the REC to supply agencies that meet certain criteria. Details of the REC and its members can be found on www.rec.co.uk.

If you have any concerns about an agency, in respect of its conduct or its compliance with the law, you should contact the Employment Agency Standards Inspectorate, which provides an enquiry line (telephone: 0845 955 5105) and investigates any complaints of this nature.

Application Forms and Documentation

Whichever route into supply teaching you choose, you will be asked to complete an application form and to attend at least one interview.

The application form will mainly relate to your personal circumstances, your qualifications, your teaching experience, your employment history and your medical history.

You are also likely to be asked to indicate your preferences in terms of the supply cover that you are prepared to provide. For example:

Preferences in terms of:

- age group

- ability level

- subjects

- specialist or general cover

- full-time or part-time

- long-term or short-term bookings

- temporary or permanent position

- how far you would be prepared to travel.

Keep in mind that the narrower your preferences the harder it might be for you to find work.

In addition to the completed application form, you will be asked to provide certain documentation to support the information that you have provided:

- proof of identification (e.g. passport, birth certificate, or new-style driving licence)

- proof of address (e.g. utility bill or bank statement)

- recent passport-sized photographs (at least two)

- a valid enhanced CRB disclosure certificate. If you do not yet have one, you will be asked to complete a disclosure application form. (If you are a teacher from overseas, you need to have a notarised copy of an equivalent check from your home country.)

- proof of qualifications (e.g. DfES letter or Certificate of Teaching Qualification or equivalent in the case of overseas teachers: see the UK National Academic Recognition Information Centre (NARIC) List to check qualifications that are deemed equivalent)

- curriculum vitae (CV)

- proof of registration with the General Teaching Council (GTC)

- references

- proof of eligibility to work in the UK.

Once you have been taken on, you will be asked to provide your P45 or P46, and your bank details. As this is to enable you to be paid, it should be one piece of information that you do not mind providing!

Criminal Records Bureau (CRB) Enhanced Disclosure

All teachers, whether working on a temporary or permanent basis, full-time or part-time, are required to have an enhanced CRB disclosure certificate.

In most cases the supply agency or local education authority (LEA) that you are hoping to work through will organise this on your behalf. They will provide you with a blank form for you to complete and will send off your form with payment. Make sure you keep a copy of the completed form.

The fee for an enhanced disclosure is £34 (at the time of writing). Most agencies and LEAs will pay this on your behalf. I have heard of some cases where the agency expects the teacher to pay for this themselves, or has deducted payment from the first salary payment. Fortunately I have never come across this myself.

In theory an enhanced CRB disclosure certificate is valid for three years (so long as you do not take a break from teaching). In reality, it seems that many agencies prefer to err on the side of caution and will ask you to complete a new form every year. If you move from one agency to another, or go on the books of more than one agency at a time, expect to complete a form for each one.

Because of the nature of the work, the post of supply teacher is exempt from the provisions of section 4 (2) of the Rehabilitation of Offenders Act 1974. This means that any criminal convictions you may have will not be treated as 'spent'. You are therefore required to declare all criminal convictions or cautions.

Failure to declare a conviction that later becomes known may result in you being excluded from the supply agency's or LEA's register, and if your supply work resulted in a contract for permanent employment at a school, you may find non-disclosure would lead to disciplinary action or even dismissal.

The information you give must be treated in confidence and only be taken into account where the offence is relevant to the post for which you are applying.

You can find out more about the CRB online at www.disclosure.gov.uk. You can also download a blank copy from this site or ring the application line on 0870 90 90 844.

The Law

Whether you are employed by a school, local education authority (LEA) or supply agency, your conduct while acting as a supply teacher must be in accordance with the child protection provisions of the Criminal Justice and Court Services Act 2000, the Education Reform Act 1988 and the Protection of Children Act 1999.

Under the Rehabilitation of Offenders Act 1974, you are required to declare all criminal convictions and cautions when applying for work in the education sector. *See* page 11 on Criminal Records Bureau enhanced disclosure for further details.

Whether you are employed directly by the school, through the LEA or a supply agency, you should have a contract outlining the specific terms and conditions relating to your employment. This is explored more fully on page 13.

If you are employed as a supply teacher through a supply agency or LEA, your legal rights and responsibilities, and those of the agency and the school(s), are outlined in the Employment Agency Act 1973 and the Conduct of Employment Agencies and Employment Businesses Regulations 2003.

If you are employed through an agency, you will find that the agency and the school will also have a contract outlining their relationship. This should include requirements concerning the school's relationship with you.

The EU Working Time Directive 2003 establishes workers' rights, including provisions that they should not be required to work more than 48 hours in a week (including overtime), and that they are entitled to up to four weeks paid holiday.

You will also be covered by the same legal protection applicable to any visitor to school premises, for example health and safety regulations and public liability.

Your Contract

Whether you work for an individual school, a local education authority (LEA) or an agency, you should be given a written contract, clearly outlining the terms and conditions of your employment.

When you sign on with an agency, a typical contract should make it clear that:

- the terms only apply to days when you are actually working for the agency

- your contract with the agency is not exclusive, which means that you can work for other agencies

- you do not have to accept any work that is offered to you

- the agency is your employer

- the agency will endeavour to obtain suitable assignments for you

- there are no guarantees that suitable work will be found

- the nature of the work is temporary.

The contract should also set out:

- the method and timing of payments

- the situation with regard to holiday pay

- the method of claiming payment, usually through the submission of a timesheet signed by an authorised member of staff at the school.

Whatever the system, make sure you keep clear and accurate records of the work you have undertaken and sign in and out on each day that you work at a school so that you have written evidence of your attendance, just in case there is any dispute.

The agency and the school will also have a contract outlining their relationship. This should include requirements concerning the school's relationship with you. You will also be covered by the same legal protection applicable to any visitor to school premises, such as public liability and health and safety regulations.

Pay

A major difference between finding supply work through schools, local education authorities (LEAs) or supply agencies is the method used to calculate your rate of pay.

Schools

All schools will pay you a day rate calculated according to the point you occupy on the teachers' pay spine.

The main difference between schools appears to be how a 'day' is interpreted. Some schools calculate your pay on the basis of the hours you have actually taught. Others will take into account the amount of hours you are actually on site. Some expect you to mark as part of the basic day. Others are prepared to pay at least a contribution in recognition of the extra time it takes you to do marking.

Payment is usually made at the end of each month. You are unlikely to be paid for holidays unless you are on a long-term contract with a single school. The school will be responsible for tax and National Insurance arrangements and any other deductions that may be required by law and which will be the responsibility of the school.

Local Education Authorities (LEAs)

LEAs will pay you a day rate relating to your pay point.

In order to calculate your daily LEA supply rate, take the appropriate annual salary relating to your pay point and divide it by 195 (that is, the number of days in a school year).

As long as you work in 26 weeks out of the possible 39 weeks in a school year, you will be eligible for an annual pay rise.

You are unlikely to be paid for holidays, unless you have worked at the same school for a whole term.

Payment is usually made monthly, one month in arrears. The LEA will be responsible for tax and National Insurance arrangements and any other deductions that may be required by law and which will be the responsibility of the LEA.

Supply Agencies

Some agencies calculate their supply teachers' pay according to the teachers' pay spine. Others will have their own scale relating to the time teachers are with the agency and the nature of their contracts (e.g. short-term, long-term). Other agencies appear to offer a flat rate, offering the same daily rate to all their teachers.

Payment is usually made weekly, one week in arrears. This is subject to deductions for tax and National Insurance, and any other deductions that may be required by law and which will be the responsibility of the agency.

Agencies are unlikely to offer payment for any time not spent on assignment, so you should not expect to be paid for absence because of illness or any other reason. However, you should be entitled to up to four weeks paid holiday.

How Long is a Day?

The length of the school day and the expectations of what the supply teacher will do in that day varies between schools, local education authorities (LEAs) and agencies, and between individual teachers. It is therefore a good idea to make sure this is discussed and agreed before accepting any bookings.

Most agencies pay a daily rate that is agreed at the start of the contract, and which applies to all schools on their books, whatever the length of day at the school and whatever the school's expectations are regarding how long you are expected to be at the school on any specific day.

Some schools and LEAs will only pay supply teachers for contact hours, which means you could be paid for as little as 5.25 hours. This does not necessarily have any correlation with the amount of time you are expected to spend on site, as the school may still expect you to come into school early and stay after lessons.

The length of a day for which you are paid should be calculated at 6.5 hours. Your hourly rate should be calculated using your gross annual salary divided by 195, then divided by 6.5.

If you are being paid for a basic 5.25-hour day, you may feel that the school should not expect you to stay at the end of the day to do marking or to attend after-school meetings. However, you may feel that if a school is paying you for a 6.5-hour day it is justified in asking you to do break duty, lesson preparation and marking.

What you consider to be acceptable is your decision, but you must make sure that the other parties involved are clear about what you will do and what you are not prepared to do before you start.

You may find that some schools will be prepared to pay a contribution on top of the basic day rate, in recognition of the additional time that you need to spend to do the work they require.

Pensions

Supply teaching is not automatically pensionable. You need to opt into the superannuation scheme in order to be eligible to receive pension contributions from your employer.

Once you have opted in, contributions are deducted from your salary. You contribute 6 per cent of your salary and your employer contributes 13.5 per cent, making a total of 19.5 per cent.

If you want to contribute to the Teachers' Superannuation Scheme, contact Teachers' Pensions at Mowden Hall, Darlington DL3 9EE, or telephone 01323 745745, and ask for Form 261.

You can also visit: www.teacherspensions.co.uk.

Unions

It has been found that supply teachers are less likely to be members of a union than any other group of teachers.

At the same time, it could be said that this group could benefit more from the support available from union membership than those on permanent and full-time contracts.

Unions offer a range of legal and professional services, including advice regarding contracts, behaviour management, insurance and pensions. They can support you in your professional development through conferences and training, and help you to keep up to date with developments in the field of education through newsletters.

The following is a list of unions for teachers:

Union	Acronym	Website
Association of Teachers and Lecturers	ATL	www.askatl.org.uk
Educational Institute of Scotland	EIS	www.eis.org.uk
National Association of Schoolmasters Union of Women Teachers	NASUWT	www.teachersunion.org.uk
National Union of Teachers	NUT	www.teachers.org.uk
Professional Association of Teachers	PAT	www.pat.org.uk
Scottish Secondary Teachers' Association	SSTA	www.ssta.org.uk
Ulster Teachers' Union	UTU	www.utu.edu

General Teaching Council (GTC)

Teachers must be registered with the General Teaching Council (GTC) in order to be able to teach in maintained schools, non-maintained special schools and Pupil Referral Units in the UK.

The requirement to register follows from the Teaching and Higher Education Act 1998.

Registration is not transferable between GTCs, so in order to be able to teach in maintained schools in England, teachers must be registered with the GTCE, with the GTCW for schools in Wales, the GTCS for Scotland or the GTCNI for Northern Ireland.

If you are a newly qualified teacher (NQT) you must register before you begin your first teaching post, whatever the nature of the post, whether permanent, part-time or supply.

Websites for each of the GTCs are as follows:

General Teaching Council for England   www.gtce.org.uk

General Teaching Council for Wales   www.gtcw.org.uk

General Teaching Council for Scotland   www.gtcs.org.uk

General Teaching Council for Northern Ireland   www.gtcni.org.uk.

Getting a Booking

Because of the nature of the work, it is more likely that you will get just an hour's notice of a booking rather than a day or a week.

One of the aspects of supply teaching that many people find hard is the need to get up and get ready for work even though you have no idea whether there will be any work for you that day. This is particularly hard in areas where there is a shortage of work.

Some examples of bookings are as follows:

You are ready and waiting. It's 7.45 a.m. The phone rings. Are you available to teach at School X? You need to be there by 8.30 a.m. It's five miles away.

You haven't had a call and it's 8.45 a.m., so you start to make plans for the day. It's 8.55 a.m. and the phone rings. Can you get to School Y? It's ten miles away. They realise you are not going to get there in time to start the first lesson, but can you get there as soon as possible?

It's 8.15 a.m. The phone rings. Can you teach at a school 30 miles away? You need to be there by 8.40 a.m.

It's 8 a.m. and the phone rings. We've got a booking for you. It's not far, it's the local Pupil Referral Unit.

It's 3.30 p.m. on Thursday afternoon. Are you available to teach all of next week? You will be covering the subject you like least.

It's 2.30 p.m. on Friday. A school ten miles away needs a teacher with your subject specialism to cover for two days next week, maybe more.

It's the agency. A school needs someone with your subject specialism to cover for four weeks.

Whatever you are offered, it is up to you whether or not you want to accept the booking. If you do not know the school, you might prefer to go in for one day before you commit to a longer-term contract.

If you would like to accept a booking but are not sure whether you will be able to get there in time, tell the agency so they can let the school decide whether or not that is acceptable. I have never lost a booking on this basis: schools are generally realistic about what is possible and prefer to know where they stand so that they can plan accordingly. This is far better than giving the impression you can get there on time and then turn up late.

Information You Need from Your Agency

Whatever the situation, the agency should be able to give you the information you need in order to be able to decide whether or not you want to take the booking.

Type of School
What sort of reputation has it got? If it has a poor reputation you might prefer just to accept a one-day booking so you can decide for yourself whether you would be happy to go back for longer.

General or Specialist Subject Cover
If it is subject specific, which subject is it? (Treat this information with caution! I have found it can change at any minute.)

Age Range
Reception, primary, secondary? If you are providing secondary school cover, you may not always be given specific information, in which case you could be covering all age groups.

Length of Contract
Not all supply cover is short term. It can be days, weeks, a term, or even longer.

Your Choice
Remember, it is up to you whether or not you accept the booking. Once you have agreed, however, you have an obligation to turn up and do your professional best.

Once you have accepted the booking you should also make sure the agency provides you with the following information:

Directions
The agency should be able to give you detailed directions. Where is the school? How far away is it? Has it got a car park? Is the school near a train, tube or bus station?

Contact Details
Make sure you get a phone number so you can ring the school if you get lost or are held up on the way. Ensure the number is one you can get through on even if you ring before school hours.

School Contact
Make sure you have the name of the cover co-ordinator, and an idea of where to find them.

Time to Arrive
What time are you expected at the school? What time do lessons start?

Getting Ready for the Day

If you have been given enough notice before the booking, it is always worth checking the school's website to find out about its ethos. Talk to colleagues to find out about its reputation. The more you know about a school before you get there, the better prepared you will be in your mind for what could be waiting for you.

What to Wear

Some schools have a dress code for staff, but in most cases how you dress tends to be determined by a combination of personal preference, the age group being taught (primary or secondary), the subject being covered and the need for comfort. The smart/casual look is probably safest: professional without being imposing.

I also recommend layers – and lots of them: you never know how efficient the school's heating is until you get there, or whether you are going to be covering ICT in a glass hothouse or PE in a muddy field.

What to Take

The list of things to take with you can be divided into two categories: things to make lessons better and things to make life at school easier.

Some ideas about the things I consider essential equipment are outlined in more detail on page 22.

While you do not want to be laden down with things, it is useful to build up a bank of material that you can use, particularly when you find yourself teaching classes where no work has been set. You will find a selection of activities at the back of this book (*see* page 91), but it is also a good idea to collect pictures, stories, poems and posters that you can use as stimulus and support material. You will find a pocket on the inside back cover where you can keep these.

How to Get There

Make sure you know what time you are expected to get to the school and aim to arrive at least ten minutes early. If you are driving, remember that school car parks can be busy in the early morning and it can be impossible to find parking. Bear in mind, too, that it can often take ten minutes to walk from the school car park to reception, and that school reception areas can be well hidden!

Essential Equipment

A few essential items can help ensure your day goes smoothly. These are mine:

Directions
School contact details
Diary
Folder (to keep information provided by school)
List of questions (to ask the school if not provided with required details)
Paper: lined and plain
Lunch
Liquid refreshment including mug, and either coffee or tea bags and milk, or thermos flask
Two old newspapers: a source of many activities, not for me to read in class!
Emergency activities (*see* page 91)
Sense of humour
Pencil case: big enough to hold all the following items:

- 10 biros

- 10 pencils (rubber topped)

- 2 rulers

- 2 pencil sharpeners

- 2 calculators

- a tube of liquid paper

- a board marker

- a piece of chalk

- a small packet of tissues.

If you have had lessons disrupted by pupils claiming they cannot start their work because they have no pens, pencils, rulers etc, you will know how useful it is to have this basic equipment. It does not involve a major investment (less than £10), but will save a lot of time.

If you do hand out anything make sure you get it back at the end of class, and count back in everything that went out, or this will become an expensive exercise. A system that I have found works well is to swap items: if pupils want to borrow anything of mine, they must give me something in return, e.g. their organiser/day planner, which they can collect back when they return my things. In schools where they do not have organisers, I have had packets of crisps, hats and even a trainer!

You may also want to mark your items in some way (a blob of bright red nail polish works well), so that it is easy to identify what is yours.

Finally, you may want to take a few 'rewards' along to hand out to mark good behaviour. Examples might include stickers or colourful biros.

On Arrival

Always arrive at the time required, preferably ten minutes before. Make sure you are clear whether the time given to you is the time school starts or the time you are expected to be there.

If there is any doubt as to whether you are going to be on time, ring the school and let them know when you expect to get there. Also ring your agency, if you are with one.

When you arrive in a new school, most schools should have the necessary information ready for you. It might be a single sheet of paper or it might be a packed folder. Hopefully, it will have all the information you need to help you provide effective cover lessons throughout your day.

The general information should include:

- the times of lessons

- a plan of the school

- a description of accepted levels of behaviour

- an outline of rewards and sanctions

- a list of members of staff you may need to contact (e.g. matron), their names and where they can be found.

Some information about the ethos of the school is also helpful.

The specific information you need should include:

- lessons to be covered: subjects, rooms, teacher whose lesson is being covered

- class details: any pupils with special needs (physical, educational or behavioural)

- a class list or register for each class

- a description of the work to be covered

- the titles of textbooks to be used, or any other source material, such as handouts

- the homework to be set and the deadline for its completion.

Inevitably, in some cases this information will not be provided, or it will not be as detailed as you would like. Do not be afraid to ask for it. It shows that you know what you are doing – and far better to sort everything out at the start of the day than to find yourself in front of a class of 30 wondering who to contact to deal with a difficult situation.

Lists of questions that you may find helpful to ask when you arrive are provided on pages 25 and 26. For a list about general areas of information *see* page 25 and for a list about more specific areas *see* page 26.

Timetable

Unfortunately for supply teachers, schools do not follow the same timetable. They start at different times, have breaks at different times, have breaks of varying lengths, and even have registration at different times of the day. This can be very difficult for the poor supply teacher who visits a different school every day.

My recommendation is to write the timetable for the day in your diary. If it is in a diary and not on a piece of paper you are less likely to lose it. It also means you have a record of the work you have done, which can be shown to the school, local education authority (LEA) or supply agency if required.

After each lesson write a few brief notes about any pupils or issues you think it would be useful to keep a record of.

If you are hoping to return to the school, it means you have a record of the classes you have covered. On your return to the school you can check back to see if you have taught a particular group before, and whether there is anything you need to take into account given your past experiences.

Bells

You may find it a good idea to check whether or not the school uses bells to signify the end of lessons. The first time I went to a school without bells I was very confused!

Most schools I have worked at use bells to signify the beginning and end of all lessons, but a few only use bells after registration and breaks, but not for every lesson. And I have been to one that gave a five-minute warning at the end of breaks.

Checklist: general

When I arrive at a school I check through the information pack (if there is one) to ensure the following is included. If not, I ask the cover co-ordinator to quickly give me the necessary information.

School Timetable
What are the start and finish times of lessons and breaks?

School Layout
A copy of a clear and up-to-date plan of the school.

Reward System
An overview of the reward system (if any) used in class to encourage good behaviour.

Disciplinary Procedure
An outline of sanctions for certain acts, e.g. swearing, chewing gum, refusing to do any work, constantly talking or distracting other pupils.

What are the stages of discipline? Are there any guidelines or procedures to be followed?

Classroom Etiquette
What is the expected procedure for pupils arriving in class?
- Enter class on arrival   Yes   No
- Wait outside class for permission to enter   Yes   No
- Other

What is the expected procedure for pupils entering the classroom?
- Sit on entering class   Yes   No
- Stand by chairs waiting for permission to sit   Yes   No
- Other

Are pupils allowed to have a drink during lessons?   Yes   No

What is the procedure if pupils wish to leave the class to:
- visit the toilet?
- go to matron?

What is the procedure if pupils have mobile phones, mp3s etc in class?

What is the procedure in the case of a fire alarm?

Checklist: specific

Class List

Please provide a class list for each period being covered.

Pupil Issues

Please identify any pupils in each class with special needs (behavioural, medical or other).

Name	Special Needs	Action

Class Lists

Schools should always provide a register for each class. Should, but unfortunately do not.

If you are not provided with a class list, at least try to find out if there are any pupils with special needs, or pupils with behavioural or other problems, before you go to the class.

If you are not provided with a class list, make your own as soon as you arrive in the class. One way to avoid being caught out by class jokers is to tell everyone to get out their organiser/day planner or any exercise book and to put it on their desk. Then go around the class taking their names from their books.

You might find it useful to make your own class list even if you are given a class register. By listing the names in relation to where the pupils are sitting, it makes it easier for you to match names to faces: by starting at the front and working your way along each row, for example. It will also give you an opportunity to have a word with the pupils as individuals.

This provides you with a register and seating plan in one, which makes it much easier when asking pupils to respond to questions. It also seems to impress pupils that you are able to match names to faces so quickly, despite having just watched you write down their names.

An alternative, if you have enough paper, is to ask the pupils to make name signs to put in front of them on their desks (although pupils can swap these around).

A further option is to invest in some labels or post-it notes and to ask the pupils to write their names on them (although this is also open to jokers writing the wrong names or swapping labels).

Registration

Many schools have computerised sheets for registration, which require you to put a horizontal pencil line through the 'p' (for present) or 'a' (for absent) against each name. Pupils who arrive late will have a line through both the 'p' and 'a'. These sheets are usually weekly and require completion during morning and afternoon registration.

The instructions at the top of the sheet clearly state that the 'p' should be crossed if pupils are present and the 'a' crossed if pupils are absent. However, some schools leave the 'p' unmarked if the pupil is present – and only cross the 'p' if the pupil is late and arrive after they have already been marked absent.

If in doubt check with the cover co-ordinator or another teacher before completing the form.

An alternative method is for teachers to complete their register electronically, using the Bromcom register, for example. This system can be used for every lesson as well as for morning and afternoon registers.

Each teacher enters an ID and a password, and selects from a list. For example:

- 1   register
- 2   gradebook
- 3   fire drill.

Once the teacher's initial and the period or class code has been entered, the register appears.

As with the previous system, 'p' is entered to indicate that pupils are present and 'a' that they are absent. You should enter an 'l' if they are late, as well as entering the number of minutes by which they are late.

You can use this system to see if pupils were in previous lessons. An underscore can be used to identify special educational needs (SEN) pupils.

Once the register is completed you press 'send' and it is electronically sent to the school office. Staff there can then phone home if needed.

Assembly

Make sure you find out whether your tutor group has got assembly, and if so, what time they need to be there, where they normally sit or stand, and whether there is anything else you need to know about the structure of assembly.

Most pupils behave quite well in assembly, but it is always worth finding out the accepted procedure in the case of misbehaviour.

Rewards and Sanctions

One of the first things I do when I arrive at a school is to find out the system of rewards and sanctions, to determine how far my authority goes in terms of administering them, and to ensure I have the necessary documentation.

Rewards

Once I have found out what the school reward system is, I do try to use it. Where appropriate, I will set criteria, e.g. offering rewards for working quietly, completing work, answering questions, and following instructions.

Possible rewards include:

- verbal praise
- positive referral
- credit/merit
- name on board
- small reward/prize.

If the school uses credits or merits or smiley faces, make sure you have a supply.

Some teachers like to offer more tangible rewards, such as sweets. You should first check the school policy on this, as sweets or chocolates may not be viewed favourably when child obesity is such a concern.

An unusual biro, multicoloured pencil or a scented rubber, all things that will be useful in the classroom, may be better alternatives. Generally the reward need not be of any great value. It is the fact that the pupil is being rewarded that makes the difference.

Sanctions

Given the unfortunate attitude of all too many pupils towards supply teachers, you really should make sure that you are clear about the school's disciplinary policy before going into a classroom.

You should also find out if there are any forms that you need to complete, such as send-out slips or detention forms, and make sure that you have the necessary paperwork.

You also need to be sure that what you consider to be suitable sanctions are acceptable to the school. For example, some schools do not like pupils to be sent out of the classroom.

You need to be clear, too, about whether you have the authority to set detention or to take any other disciplinary action and, if you do, what the correct procedure is. You do not want to threaten detention, only to find out that this is not allowed by the school.

Possible sanctions include:

- verbal reprimand
- moving a pupil/pupils away from classmates
- telling a pupil to stand outside
- talking to a pupil outside the classroom
- sending a pupil to another classroom
- writing comments in the pupil's day book/organiser/diary
- reporting a pupil's/pupils' behaviour to the class teacher/form tutor/head of year
- detention during break
- detention after school.

Good and Bad Lists

I have my own system for encouraging good behaviour, which I find works particularly well with younger and lower-ability pupils and which has stood me in good stead when I have been unable to get clear information from the school about their system.

I begin by telling the class that they will all be put on to the good list and that during the course of the lesson, depending on their behaviour, they will either stay on the good list or move to neutral and then the bad list. They can also move back on to the neutral and good list if their behaviour improves. At the end of the lesson everyone on the good list can be congratulated and those on the bad list can be made aware of your disappointment.

The list is passed on to the teacher whose lesson is being covered, and it is up to them whether they wish to reward those on the good list or impose sanctions on those on the bad list.

By placing every pupil on the good list initially, it means everyone starts on an equal footing. It also means that the ones who work quietly but without standing out do not get passed over for praise or reward.

I have always found pupils to be very keen to know which list they are on at the end of the lesson – even when there is no tangible reward to be gained.

Class Discipline

For a supply teacher, every day at a new school is like the first day of term. You do not know the pupils – and they do not know you.

Many will be testing you, looking for signs of weakness, playing on your lack of knowledge of the school and its policies.

You may also have the added problem that until you walk into the classroom you do not even know what you are going to be teaching.

How do you cope?

Every class will be different, but the following suggestions may be helpful:

- First impressions might never be so important. The first five minutes could make the difference between 60 minutes of frustration or 60 minutes of reasonable calm.

- Try to get the pupils to line up quietly outside the classroom. Allow them to enter the classroom in small groups.

- Begin by introducing yourself: write your name on the board.

- If they haven't already done so, tell the pupils to prepare themselves for the lesson (pens and books out, coats off, bags on floor etc).

- Take the register.

- Write a short activity on the board (if you can do this before the pupils come into the class even better). The teacher whose lesson it is may have left one, you may have your own favourites, or you can find a selection of suitable activities listed at the back of the book (*see* pages 91–138). These will act as either ice-breakers or settlers, and will also give you time to read through and familiarise yourself with the work that has been left by the teacher.

- Have spare pens, pencils and paper at the ready for those who need it (*see* Essential Equipment, page 22).

- Once you are ready to set the work for the lesson, ensure the class is quiet before explaining the work pupils are to do.

- Although not ideal, you might prefer to send a disruptive pupil to stand outside the door* while you are explaining the work to the rest of the class, rather than have your explanation constantly interrupted. Once the class has settled down to work, you can deal with the pupil outside the room.

- At the end of the lesson, stand by the door as the pupils leave. Make sure they leave the classroom in an orderly fashion. Praise pupils who have behaved well and/or worked well.

Be sure this is acceptable to the school.

Do Not Make Assumptions

You do not know this class – and they do not know you.

If you can see pupils continually talking or messing about, do not assume that they are troublemakers – try to find out what the problem is. It could be that they do not understand what they are supposed to do and are too shy to ask you, or they could have Attention Deficit Hyperactivity Disorder (ADHD) or another condition.

Once the work has been set and explained to the group as a whole, you have the opportunity to walk around the class and talk to individuals, to make sure they understand the work and to help them if they have not understood what they should be doing.

Schools do not appreciate lazy supply teachers who set the work and then just sit back and wait for the end of the lesson. Why should they? Circulate around the room, talk to the pupils, discuss their work with them, make sure they are clear about what they should be doing and have understood your instructions.

The fact that you are walking around the room should also help you to keep control.

Talk to the Staff

I have had classes where I have walked out at the end feeling a total failure.

Then, letting off steam in the staff room, I have discovered that everyone has problems with that particular class. I could have kept quiet, not wanting to admit my failure, but by being open and sharing my concerns, I have ended up feeling much better.

Perhaps the worst aspect of being a supply teacher is the feeling of isolation. You can have days when you walk into the school, get handed your timetable at reception, and that is the last adult contact you have all day.

In some schools there will be nothing you can do about this. In others it is simply down to you to start a conversation with people. When you arrive, ask if there are other supply teachers at the school. At break or lunch, go to the staff room, sit down with other teachers and ask them about the school, or ask them if they have any tips for dealing with Class 8X or whatever group you have that afternoon.

If you sit on your own in a corner reading a book, then you should not complain if no one speaks to you. There is no reason why the school staff should talk to you. They do not know who you are, why you are in the school, or how long you will be there. It is up to you to make the first move.

Cover Work

In my experience most schools operate a system where the cover work is taped to the desk in the classroom where the cover is to take place.

This is not a bad system, but it does mean that if the work has not been left, you do not find out until you are actually in the classroom in front of the pupils. There may be some classes you feel you can leave while you go to find work, but this is obviously not an ideal situation. And anyway, where do you go to find the work?

Teachers are supposed to provide work for cover teachers to give to their classes while they are absent, but it is not always possible for this to be organised, and even if the work has been left, it is easy for it to go astray. So you will find it very helpful to build up a bank of activities that you can give to pupils when this situation arises.

You will find some ideas provided at the back of this book (*see* pages 91–138). As you will see, there is a general section, with suggested activities that can be related to almost any subject, followed by subject-specific activities. Although these activities are essentially time-fillers, they all have some educational value.

As it is not usually until you are actually in the classroom with the class that you realise the need for a time-filler, the majority of the emergency activities provided can be introduced to the class without the need for any special equipment.

Problems at the School

We have all heard horror stories about supply teachers being given the same seemingly out-of-control group over and over again, with no support from the school management. In this case, what do you do?

Talk to the staff at the school. They are being unfair to you and to the pupils. See if there is a way that you can resolve this between you.

If You are Employed by an Agency

If you are with an agency, check the details of your contract. Check through the paperwork that they provided when you signed up with them. Some may provide very clear outlines as to the procedure to follow.

If you do not feel that the school is providing adequate support, the next step should be to talk to the agency. Find out if they knew the situation at that school before they sent you there. If they were aware of the situation, find out why they did not say anything. Ask them for their suggestion as to what should happen next. Try to find a solution within the terms of your contract.

Good agencies will be as concerned about your satisfaction with the work being found for you as with the satisfaction of the school. Remember, you are under no obligation to return to a school, unless you have made a commitment for a specific period of time. In this case, you need to be sure that you have a valid reason for not returning to the school, and that your dissatisfaction will not lead to you finding yourself without work and unlikely to be found any new work by a disgruntled agency.

If You are Employed by a School or Local Education Authority (LEA)

Talk to your union representative. The fact that you are at the school on a supply contract does not affect your rights as a teacher.

More Problems at the School

In the same way that we have all heard horror stories about schools, we have all heard horror stories about supply teachers. To avoid such stories being told about you, ensure you follow this basic list of things to do.

This first list is based on common sense and professional courtesy:

- turn up

- turn up on time: for the booking, and to each lesson

- dress in a professional manner

- keep in regular contact with your agency, if applicable

- let your agency know if you are not going to be available

- if you are unavoidably delayed and are going to be late, ring the school and the agency

- work with and involve support staff.

Everything in the following list relates to real situations, unbelievable though they may seem:

- do not read a book, magazine or newspaper in front of a class

- do not sit with your feet up on the front desk while your class is getting out of control

- do not eat in class

- do not swear at pupils

- do not leave the school part way through the day without letting anyone know

- do not drink alcohol immediately before or during your working day

- do not hit pupils.

End of the Day

When you leave a school at the end of the day make sure you:

- have completed all the paperwork required and have returned all items to where they belong

- have completed any marking you agreed to do

- sign out at reception

- put any classwork you have collected in the appropriate class teacher's pigeon hole or wherever you have been asked to leave it

- leave a note for each teacher regarding class behaviour, action taken and any issues arising

- leave each classroom in the condition you found it (however tempting it is to rearrange it!)

- return your supply teacher's handbook and pack as required

- return any keys/equipment provided for the day to the appropriate place or person

- complete and return the school's evaluation sheet.

- take everything of yours away with you

Agency Teachers

- Get your timesheet signed if it is a one-day booking* (if it is longer term, get it signed at the end of the assignment, or each week, as appropriate).

- Fax or post your claim form to your agency.

- Ring your agency if there are any issues arising from the day that you need to inform them about.

* It is important to submit your timesheets as soon as possible, as any delay can affect invoicing.

Newly Qualified Teachers (NQTs)

Working as a supply teacher instead of going straight into full-time employment may not be everyone's choice, but it can have many benefits. It is a way of working at a number of schools without making a long-term commitment, enabling you to decide whether or not these are schools you would like to work at in the longer term. It also enables you to experiment with different teaching techniques in different schools.

However, once you have started work as a supply teacher there are some limits regarding your induction period.

If you are an NQT working as a supply teacher, you must spend at least one term at a school in order for it to count towards your induction period.

Time spent as a supply teacher cannot be counted retrospectively, so it is a good idea to try to find out from your head teacher exactly how long you are likely to be needed at the school. Most supply teachers would be pleased to find a short-term contract extended, but it would be frustrating for you to find that you have ended up spending a year at a school without being able to count any of it towards your induction period.

NQTs can work as supply teachers without having served their induction period for up to four terms. After this time, you are not allowed to work as a supply teacher unless the placements are part of your induction.

The local education authority (LEA) may, in certain circumstances, be able to extend this period, but this would only be in exceptional circumstances.

Special Needs

As a supply teacher you will inevitably be asked to cover classes that include pupils with special needs. You may also have the opportunity to teach at special schools.

The term 'special needs' covers a wide range and degree of physical, learning and behavioural conditions.

You do not have to have specific qualifications or be specially trained to work with special-needs pupils in a supply-teacher capacity, but most schools, local education authorities (LEAs) and agencies will require you to have experience if you are going to be working specifically with special-needs classes.

In a special school, class numbers should be smaller, and more detailed information about individual pupils should be available than would be possible with mainstream classes.

Whether you are working in a mainstream or a special school, it is advisable to find out as much as you can about the individual pupils, their strengths and difficulties, and whether there are any recommendations about how to deal with specific situations. Some examples of useful information are as follows:

- If you need to use any special equipment that you have not used before, for example a radio aid if you have a child with hearing difficulties, try to get an explanation of how to use it and practise using it before you go into the class.

- Find out whether you will have a teaching assistant (TA) or learning support assistant (LSA) with you. If possible, have a word with them before going into class. They should be able to give you a useful insight into the pupils' behaviour, ability and attitude. If you have been able to establish what you plan to do with the class, it will help the TA or LSA if you can brief them beforehand. If they are good at their job you will find their support to you as a supply teacher invaluable.

- Make sure you are aware of any medical information you should know about.

- Be sure that you are aware of understanding, language and behaviour issues.

Eligibility to Work in the United Kingdom

If you have a British or EU passport, you can work in the UK without restrictions. If not, you may find that there are limitations on the type of work you are able to do, or the length of time you are allowed to work in the UK.

The rules relating to visas and work permits are subject to frequent change. This means it is essential that, if you are hoping to work as a teacher in the UK, you should start by contacting the British Embassy, British Consulate or British High Commission in your home country to find out the most up-to-date and accurate information regarding your eligibility to work here. Failure to do so could lead to delays and added expense. Whatever happens, do not sign any contracts for jobs or make any other legally binding commitment before receiving confirmation of the terms under which you are entitled to work in the UK.

The following information is provided for guidance only. It is not intended to provide comprehensive coverage.

European Economic Area (EEA)*

If you are an EEA national or Swiss national you have a right to work in the UK. You do not need a work permit but may be required to register under the Worker Registration Scheme if you are from the Czech Republic, Estonia, Hungary, Latvia, Lithuania, Poland, Slovakia or Slovenia.

British Spouse

You are entitled to work in the UK if you are accompanying your spouse, who is a British or EU national. You do not need a work permit, but must have a settlement visa or EEA family permit.

Commonwealth Teachers

If you are a teacher from the Commonwealth you may have the 'right to abode' in the UK, which means you can live and work in the UK without restriction. If not, you may be eligible for one of the following:

- **A Working Holidaymaker Visa**

This visa allows you to live in the UK for up to two years and to work in the UK for up to 12 months. To qualify for this you need to be under the age of 30. You must be able to show that you are mainly here on holiday and that you can finance your holiday and return home without the need to work. You are not allowed to take contracts of longer than four months. Once your working holidaymaker visa has expired, you would only be permitted to continue working in the UK if eligible to switch into work-permit employment.

- **British Ancestry Visa**

If you are a Commonwealth citizen with a British parent or grandparent, you are eligible for a UK ancestry visa, which means you can work in the UK for up to five years. You do not need a work permit.

Foreign Nationals

As a foreign national, unless you qualify under the permit-free employment scheme (*see* below), you must have a valid work permit to work in the UK. Only a school that has offered you a contract lasting at least four months can apply for this and if granted, you can then work for that school for up to four years. You cannot apply for a work permit yourself, nor can a supply agency apply for one on your behalf. You will not be granted a work permit for casual supply work.

Permit-free Employment

If you are a teacher coming to the UK under an approved exchange scheme, you will not need a work permit as this is one of the categories under permit-free employment.

For contact details for your nearest British Mission Overseas, or further information concerning your eligibility to work in the UK, visit www.ukvisas.gov.uk, www.homeoffice.gov.uk or www.workingintheuk.gov.uk.

*EEA countries include: Austria, Belgium, Denmark, Finland, France, Germany, Greece, Iceland, Ireland, Italy, Liechtenstein, Luxembourg, the Netherlands, Norway, Portugal, Spain, Sweden and the United Kingdom.

Teachers from Abroad

For general information about what you need to become a supply teacher in the UK, *see* page 5. If you do not hold a British passport or you qualified abroad, you will also need to check the following details concerning qualifications and documentation.

Qualifications

In order to be able to work as a teacher in the UK, you will need to have trained and qualified as a teacher in your home country.

If you are recognised as a qualified teacher in any European Economic Area (EEA)* member state, your qualifications should be recognised in the UK, and you should be able to apply for Qualified Teacher Status (QTS) without the need for further training.

If you trained and qualified as a teacher outside the EEA and are not a national of an EEA member state, you can still work for up to four years in the UK as a supply teacher, without the need for QTS.

If you have qualified abroad, you will need to be able to prove that you have:

- teaching qualifications that are equivalent to UK standards. If in any doubt, contact the UK National Academic Recognition Information Centre (NARIC), which is the official provider of information on the comparability of international qualifications. Its website address is www.naric.org.uk.

- undertaken a check in your home country equivalent to the CRB enhanced disclosure (*see* page 11)

- the legal right to work in the United Kingdom.

Documentation

Your agency and/or school will usually want to see originals, or certified copies, of the following documentation. You should not assume that photocopies will be acceptable:

- your work permit or visa

- your qualifications

- at least two references

- a medical certificate

- a national police reference

- your passport

- proof of address (e.g. a recent bank statement)

- two or more passport photographs.

EEA countries include: Austria, Belgium, Denmark, Finland, France, Germany, Greece, Iceland, Ireland, Italy, Liechtenstein, Luxembourg, the Netherlands, Norway, Portugal, Spain, Sweden and the United Kingdom.

THE SCHOOL COVER CO-ORDINATOR

What Makes a Good Cover Co-ordinator?

Every school will have someone who is responsible for organising cover for absent members of staff. In small primary schools this may be the head teacher, while in large secondary schools this may be a senior member of staff.

In some cases they may not have a specific title, in others they may be known as the supply co-ordinator or the cover co-ordinator. Throughout this book we have used the term cover co-ordinator.

So, what makes a good cover co-ordinator? The answer to this question will depend on who you are talking to: the school, the agency, the teachers or the supply teachers.

From the school's point of view, a good cover co-ordinator is someone who always ensures that appropriate cover is provided whenever it is needed, but does not have a staff room full of supply teachers doing nothing. The school will also be concerned that the quality of cover is high, but is kept within budget.

The agency will appreciate a cover co-ordinator who is able to give as much notice as possible, and provide clear and comprehensive information about the cover required. It will also appreciate dealing with someone who returns calls, ensures invoices are paid, and provides feedback (positive and negative) on its teachers.

The teacher's view of what makes a good cover co-ordinator will depend on whether they are looking at it from the point of view of someone whose lesson is being covered or someone who is hoping they will not lose their non-contact period. If it is the former, they will hope that the co-ordinator will find someone to cover their class who is able to control their class and deliver the lesson as described in their cover details. If it is the latter, their ideal cover co-ordinator will be someone who always gets someone else to do the cover and not them!

A supply teacher will give top marks to someone who has a user-friendly, easy-to-understand system, which means they can easily see where they have to be, when, and covering which subject. They will also be looking for someone who is welcoming and supportive and who can provide the information they need to do a professional job.

Why Hire Supply Teachers?

Supply teachers provide a valuable and flexible service to schools.

When teachers are absent, because of illness, INSET, school trips or for any other reason, you have a limited number of choices as to how to cover their lessons.

Your options will depend to an extent on the nature of the absence. Long-term absences should be covered by a qualified teacher, but some schools now consider it acceptable for short-term absences to be covered by a cover supervisor or a higher-level teaching assistant (HLTA).

Your options are therefore to:

- ask a member of your permanent teaching staff to cover lessons

- use cover supervisors or other suitably experienced and trained support staff

- use a supply teacher to cover lessons.

We all know how valuable non-contact periods are to teachers. To lose even one in a week can be disappointing, to lose more can seriously disrupt a teacher's plans, and add pressure to an already stressful job.

The Remodelling Cover Recommendations produced by the Workforce Monitoring Agreement Group state that teachers can only be asked to provide up to 38 hours cover in a year, and that efforts should be made to ensure that it is much less than this.

Cover supervisors and HLTAs should only be considered for short-term absences. They are not qualified to teach and should not be asked to do so.

As a result, unless your school's teachers are going to be asked to turn down opportunities for professional development in school time, and be expected to struggle into work however ill they are, you will need to use a supply teacher.

Supply cover can be anything from:

- the instant fix – someone to cover a day of lessons at short notice

- the familiar face – someone who is regularly booked to cover a variety of needs

- the permanent plug – someone booked to cover longer-term absence.

A good supply teacher can meet the demands of any of these types of bookings. Most have a professional attitude and will be keen to do a good job. It is obviously in the school's interests for a good cover co-ordinator to do what they can to make it easier for the supply teacher to do so.

Some suggestions about how this can be achieved are outlined in the following pages. Many of you will think these are simply common sense. They are, but perhaps that is why they are so often taken for granted and forgotten.

Where to Find Supply Teachers

Having identified the need for a supply teacher, you now need to decide how you are going to find the right one for your school. There are effectively three sources you can use. All have advantages. The decision as to which will be used is usually down to availability of appropriately qualified staff, confidence in the quality of service provided, and cost.

School Pool

In some cases schools will have their own pool of teachers who can be called upon to provide supply cover. This is often made up of teachers who have taken early retirement from the school or have gone part-time, but are prepared to step in to provide cover on a short-term, ad-hoc basis. It might also include teachers who have contacted the school on spec.

Under this system the teacher is an employee of the school. The school will be responsible for interviewing the teacher, ensuring all the paperwork, including the CRB disclosure, is up to date and in order, and for agreeing rates of pay. Supply teachers employed directly by the school are subject to tax and National Insurance under the school PAYE arrangements.

Local Education Authority (LEA) List

In some counties the LEA has a register of potential supply teachers that it makes available to schools in its area. This will include relevant contact details so schools can book teachers from the list.

With this system the teacher is an employee of the LEA and may work for different schools from day to day. The LEA is responsible for interviewing the teacher, organising a CRB check and ensuring that all paperwork is in order. The LEA agrees the rate of pay and is responsible for making salary payments, for tax and National Insurance arrangements.

This system is not available in all counties. Some LEAs use commercial supply agencies.

Supply Agencies

Many supply teachers register for work with employment or supply agencies. Most supply agencies are commercial organisations that operate to make a profit. They charge the school for providing appropriate supply teachers. As such, the supply teachers are employees of the agencies. The agencies are responsible for all the legal checks, interviews and salary payments. The agency will invoice the school for work undertaken by its supply teachers. The fee charged to the school will include a percentage for the agency.

Supply teachers recruited by schools through employment and supply agencies are not considered to be employed by the LEA or a school governing body. As such they do not meet the definition of a school teacher in the School Teachers' Pay and Conditions Act 1991 and are therefore not subject to the provisions of that Act. This is also relevant to tax and National Insurance. Supply agencies are responsible for tax and National Insurance payments for the supply teachers they provide.

Working with Individual Teachers

There are many benefits to building up your own pool of teachers. These will usually be people who are known to you and the pupils, who will have taught at the school before taking early retirement or going part-time. They will be familiar with the school, its layout, ethos and procedures and policies.

There are also a few disadvantages. If you need someone at short notice, you will be responsible for ringing around your pool of teachers until you find someone who is available. This can be very time consuming.

These teachers may also be unwilling or unable to teach more than a limited number of days per week.

Where the school recruits supply teachers from its own contacts, it is responsible for interviewing them and ensuring that the necessary checks are undertaken. If the results are not known before the teacher starts work, the school is responsible for ensuring effective supervision is organised.

The checks relate to identity, permission to work, qualifications, health, references, barred teachers (DfES List 99) and criminal records.

If you are looking to fill longer-term or potentially permanent positions you may find it useful to use your local education authority (LEA) or a supply agency, in order to introduce new and potentially permanent staff into your school.

Self-employed Supply Teachers

Some supply teachers may have registered themselves as self-employed. This means that they are responsible for making their own arrangements for tax and National Insurance. Although you are not obliged to check on this, it is worth making sure you are clear about the situation so there is no risk of the school being asked to make back-dated employer contributions. (For further information, contact your tax office or social security office.)

Working with the Local Education Authority (LEA)

Different systems operate in different counties.

LEA Registers

In some areas schools can access a register of available supply teachers, which is maintained by the LEA.

The LEA will undertake the necessary checks and interviews before adding teachers' names to the list, although the school is free to arrange a further interview if required.

The LEA will usually provide schools with a password, which can be used to access the register, usually held on a secure internet site, where you will find information about the teachers' experience, subject specialism and contact details. You can then contact anyone on the list to book them.

In this situation the supply teacher will be paid via the LEA payroll, on the basis of information submitted by the school(s). Supply teachers employed by the LEA are subject to tax and NI under the LEA PAYE arrangements.

Other than the initial stages involved in assessing the teachers' suitability to be included on the county register, the LEA does not generally become actively involved.

In some counties, the LEA is not directly involved in the area of supply cover, but may recommend a commercial agency operating in the area. In others, the county council prefers to direct enquiries towards supply agencies operating via the internet.

The responsibility for completing the claim form for time spent teaching at the school may be the school's responsibility or it may be the supply teacher's. If it is the school's responsibility, you will need to establish the teacher's payroll or personnel number. If it is the teacher's responsibility, it is likely that you will still need to sign the claim form, so it would be helpful if the supply teacher knows where to find you (or anyone else with authority to sign) at the end of the school day.

Working with Supply Agencies

A supply agency is essentially an employment agency, specifically geared to the education sector. Its aim is to provide schools with temporary staff and to provide the teachers on its books with employment.

The ultimate target of any employment agency will be to try to fill all the places required by its schools and to find employment for all its available teachers. Wherever possible, the better agencies will try to ensure that schools and teachers are well matched, by providing subject specialists where required, for example.

For schools, the key to achieving the best possible service from their supply agency has to be good communication. The more information the agency has about your school and its requirements, the better able it will be to find the right supply teacher. In addition, the more notice you can give to the agency, the more likely it is that it will be able to match your requirements.

If you are responsible for organising cover in your school, you need to be able to provide the appropriate information. You may be tempted to paint a rose-tinted picture of your pupils' behaviour and academic levels. This is unlikely to get you the best supply teacher for the job – and could cause you, the supply teacher and the agency problems.

Any good supply agency will want to visit your school and meet you. You will probably find that the agency has one main point of contact who acts as co-ordinator or consultant for your school. It is certainly in your interests to invite them to your school: it can help the agency brief a teacher if it has some first-hand experience of the school. And most people find it easier to deal with a person they have met, rather than one they have only spoken to on the phone.

In the same way that supply agencies are competing to be asked to find teachers, the schools are competing for the best supply teachers, so it does no harm to do everything you can to build a good working relationship with your agency. This doesn't necessarily need much effort. Returning calls, paying the agency's invoices on time, and providing feedback on the teachers supplied – good or bad – will all be appreciated.

There is nothing to stop you using more than one agency, which can be a useful way to compare the service provided. Many schools will have a preferred agency, but will go to others if that agency is unable to help.

When deciding which agency to choose it can be useful to find out about the experiences of other schools. Also look at costs, terms and conditions, and terms of business (e.g. does the agency charge if you wish to take on a supply teacher on a permanent contract?).

It can also be useful to find out whether the agency is a member of the industry's self-regulatory body, the Recruitment and Employment Confederation (*see* page 143 for further details or visit www.rec.co.uk) and whether it has been awarded a Quality Mark.

If your supply teachers are being provided by an agency, it is the agency's responsibility to undertake the necessary checks with regard to identity, permission to work, qualifications, health, references, barred teachers and criminal records. However, the school is still responsible for ensuring that these checks have been completed, in which case you may wish to ask the agency to provide a written assurance that the necessary checks have been carried out, and a list of the checks undertaken.

The Law

As cover co-ordinator, it will be useful for you to know something about the law relating to supply teachers, particularly with regard to your school's rights and the legal relationship between your school, the supply teacher and the agency.

The *Use of Supply Teachers Circular 7/96* gives guidance on the legal requirements relevant to the use of supply teachers, including the checks that must be carried out when recruiting them, and related issues. It also provides a list of government contacts.

If your school employs supply teachers from its own contacts, without going through the local education authority (LEA) or a supply agency, the legal relationship will be that of employer and employee, and your rights and the employee's rights will be the same as between the school and the permanent teaching staff.

Supply teachers and schools that do use the services of LEAs and supply agencies are protected by the Employment Agency Act 1973 and the Conduct of Employment Agencies and Employment Business Regulations 2003.

According to these regulations, it is the responsibility of the supply agency or LEA to obtain sufficient information from the school to enable it to provide a suitable teacher. For example, they should ask you about the dates and duration of the work, the type of work, and whether any special qualifications or experience are required.

It is also the agency or LEA's responsibility to confirm the identity of the supply teacher, and to confirm their qualifications, experience and training. This includes obtaining copies of any relevant qualifications and obtaining two references. Copies should be made available to the school, if required. You should, therefore, be able to take it for granted that all the necessary checks have been undertaken, including obtaining a CRB enhanced disclosure. This said, it does not do any harm to make sure all the paperwork is in order, especially when working with an agency for the first time.

If the agency or LEA is a member of the self-regulatory body for the industry, the Recruitment and Employment Confederation (REC), they should adhere to its Code of Conduct (*see* page 143 or www.rec.co.uk for further information).

All supply teachers should have a Contract for Services, provided by the supply agency, which outlines the contract existing between the agency and the employee. This will cover such issues as professional behaviour and notice required. As the agency is the employer, any concerns relating to the supply teacher's job performance or professional behaviour should be referred to the agency.

Additional terms may be outlined in the contract made between the school and the agency, for example in terms of notice required for cancellations. These are agreed at the discretion of the parties involved.

The legal responsibility between the school and the supply teacher is largely as it would be between the school and any visitor to the school, for example in terms of health and safety (*see* page 62 for details concerning insurance).

Supply Teachers' Qualifications

Before employing a supply teacher in your school you must be sure that they are suitably qualified and legally entitled to work in the UK. If you are employing a teacher through a supply agency or local education authority (LEA), these checks should have been undertaken before the teacher was recommended to you. If in any doubt, you should ask for a letter from the LEA or agency detailing the checks and confirming that they have been undertaken.

If the school is employing the teacher directly, it is legally responsible for ensuring that the teacher has:

- Qualified Teacher Status (QTS)

- a relevant teaching qualification (or equivalent)

- the health and physical capacity for such employment.

Schools are also legally obliged to check the Department for Education and Skills (DfES) List 99 and the Department of Health (DoH) Protection of Children Act List (POCAL), or the Scottish equivalent: the Protection of Children (Scotland) Act, before employing a supply teacher, as it is unlawful to employ anyone in a post from which they are barred. If it is found that the teacher is not totally barred, but is subject to restrictions on their employment, under no circumstances should they be placed in a post that would in any way infringe those restrictions.

Copies of List 99 are usually held by the LEA, further education organisations and associations representing independent schools. If your school does not have access to the latest list, you can write to the DfES quoting the teacher's full name, date of birth and, if they have one, their DfES reference number. Urgent requests can be made by fax.

Where a teacher is not used continuously, you should repeat the check annually.

More information on this can be found on DfES Circular 11/95: Misconduct of Teachers and Workers with Children and Young Persons and in *The Protection of Children Act 1999: A Practical Guide to the Act for all Organisations Working with Children*.

Although the regulations relating to QTS do not apply to independent schools, the responsibilities are the same as for maintained schools in relation to health, barring and criminal records. The school should ensure that all relevant checks are carried out.

Eligibility to Work in the United Kingdom

If a supply teacher has a British or EU passport, they can work in the UK without restrictions. If this is not the case, there may be limitations on the type of work they are entitled to do, the length of time they are allowed to work in your school and the length of time they are allowed to stay in the UK.

As the rules relating to visas and permits can change at any time, it is important to ensure you have the most up-to-date information concerning eligibility to work in schools in the UK. This can be found on the Home Office website www.homeoffice.gov.uk, or visit www.ukvisas.gov.uk or www.workingintheuk.gov.uk.

The nature of a teacher's entitlement to work in the UK will depend on whether they are from the European Economic Area (EEA)*, the Commonwealth or whether they are a foreign national.

In each case, you should ask to see originals, or certified copies, of the following documentation:

- work permit or visa

- passport

- national police reference

- qualifications

- medical certificate

- references

- passport photographs

- proof of address.

A teacher who has qualified abroad will need to prove that their qualifications are equivalent to UK standards. If you are in any doubt, you can contact the UK National Academic Recognition Information Centre (NARIC) on www.naric.org.uk. This is the official provider of information on the comparability of international qualifications.

European Economic Area (EEA)*

If the teacher is an EEA national or Swiss national they have a right to work in the UK. They do not need a work permit, but may be required to register under the Worker Registration Scheme if they are from the Czech Republic, Estonia, Hungary, Latvia, Lithuania, Poland, Slovakia or Slovenia.

Commonwealth Teachers

If the teacher is from the Commonwealth, they may be working in the UK on a UK ancestry visa, which means they can work in the UK for up to five years. There is no limit on the length of their contract with your school within this time.

Alternatively, they may be working in the UK on a working holidaymaker visa. This means that they are only allowed to work for up to half the time they are living in the UK (up to a maximum of 12 months of a two-year stay). They are not allowed to take a contract lasting more than four months with your school.

Foreign Nationals

A school planning to employ a teacher who is a foreign national, is responsible for applying for their work permit. Their contract with the school can be for anything between four months and four years.

*EEA countries include: Austria, Belgium, Denmark, Finland, France, Germany, Greece, Iceland, Ireland, Italy, Liechtenstein, Luxembourg, the Netherlands, Norway, Portugal, Spain, Sweden and the United Kingdom.

Helping Your Supply Teachers to Help You

Being a supply teacher going into a school for the first time is like starting a new job – only without an interview, induction day or introductions.

Most supply teachers want to do a good job – but they do need a bit of support if they are going to have a chance to do their best.

This is a list of things I hope to receive when I arrive at a new school:

- my timetable for the day – with subjects, room numbers and absent teachers' names

- a description of the school day – lesson times, breaks, registration times

- lesson plans for each class to be covered

- class lists for each class to be covered – and information about any pupils with special needs

- a brief description of the school's reward and sanction system – and the necessary paperwork

- information about where to find registers – if I am covering registration

- a map of the school – preferably up to date – with clearly marked blocks/rooms

- a brief description of school and classroom etiquette

- a list of staff I can go to for assistance – and where I can find them

- directions to the staff room, toilets and tea-making facilities

- information about health and safety issues – e.g. fire drill and where to find matron

- a key to any rooms likely to be locked (or information on where to find key)

- a pack of equipment – whiteboard pens, biros, pencils, rulers, rubbers, paper

- a few words of welcome and a friendly smile.

Briefing Your Supply Teachers

The quality of cover provided by a supply teacher will be significantly affected by the quality of the briefing the school is able to provide them with.

Senior staff in a school would not be impressed with teachers who went into their classrooms unprepared, and yet they can force this situation on to supply teachers, simply because of a lack of forethought.

Supply teachers generally have a limited amount of time to prepare themselves for the day ahead, so please make sure they are given the essential information that will help them get to the right place at the right time with the information they need to deliver an appropriate lesson

I have been handed a 40-page Supply Teacher's Handbook, with no contents page, that described the school's history, the latest Ofsted report, gave a full list of staff, including the cleaners, and listed the school governors, before giving the daily timetable and map of the school. I was constantly being told to refer to other pages for further information (which would have been a lot easier if there had been page numbers) or to ask the appropriate faculty heads or subject co-ordinators (which would have been fine if I knew where to find them). I have also been to a school where I was given a list of subjects with room numbers – and nothing else – not even the times of lessons or a map showing where I could find the classrooms.

Supply teachers need information about the lessons they are required to cover, and the classes, in order to be able to do their job properly. They will also benefit from information about policies regarding discipline, sanctions and rewards, and the names of senior staff. Any other information should follow this essential information. For example, they do not need to receive a detailed history of the school in order to be able to teach there, but it does help if they can be given some idea of the school's ethos.

To help the briefing process some ideas for a supply teachers' handbook have been provided (*see* page 61), which could be used or adapted to suit your situation. Although there are quite a few points on the list, once the information has been provided this could be adapted into a standard handbook or information sheet to be given to all supply teachers.

Welcome

As cover co-ordinator, you can do a lot to ensure that your supply teachers feel welcome and will want to return. I personally would prefer to go back to a school where the pupils' behaviour leaves something to be desired but the staff are friendly and supportive, than one where the pupils are well behaved but I am ignored in the staff room.

The supply teacher will be in your school because you have invited them there. They have come to provide a necessary and valuable service. Yet so many supply teachers have stories of feeling unwelcome or of being viewed as a necessary evil. We do not expect everyone to fall at our feet, but it is nice to be recognised and welcomed as a visiting professional and colleague.

I know the supply teacher might only be booked at your school for one day, and that everyone else may be under pressure, but a hello and a smile from just one person can make quite a difference. So, although no one is expecting schools to organise a welcoming committee, a pleasant greeting from the cover co-ordinator can go a long way.

Cover Work

Any supply teacher with a professional attitude towards their work will want to familiarise themselves as much as possible with the work they will be required to do.

I have come across a variety of systems for leaving cover work. The most common seems to be to leave it on the desk in the appropriate classroom. This system has its merits, and generally works well. The disadvantages are that the teacher providing cover does not see it until they enter the classroom, which is usually at the same time as the pupils. This means that they have no time to prepare, or to check any ambiguities. This is not a problem if the class being covered is a well-behaved one, but can be problematic if the pupils are difficult to settle.

Another problem with this system is that the teacher has no idea whether or not the work will be there until they arrive in the class. I have had countless cases where no work has been left, or the teacher covering the previous class took it with them by mistake. I have also, after a long search, found it hidden in a drawer (so the pupils could not find it), and thrown in the bin (by the pupils who did find it!). I have also arrived in class only to find a note to say the work has been left in the staff room.

My ideal system would be to have a cover tray in the staff room, where all the work for the day can be found first thing in the morning. This way all the teachers doing cover lessons can collect it all in the morning and have a chance to look through it before lessons begin. If there are any ambiguities, they at least have a chance to find someone who might be able to clarify them. If there is any work missing, they have time to find the head of department or, failing that, to think of something for the class to do, such as the ideas listed at the back of this book (*see* pages 91–138).

On too many occasions I have arrived in class to find that there has been no work left, and other times when the quality of the work set has left me wondering why the teacher bothered. I have been left everything from a few (often illegible) lines scribbled on a page, to immaculately typed notes detailing learning objectives, starter, introduction, development work, the names of responsible pupils and pupils to look out for.

A template combining elements of the best examples can be found on page 60.

Discipline

I once went to a school where, when I asked about disciplinary procedures and sanctions, was told there was no need for them. There may be some schools where this is true, but I have not yet come across any of them.

In any case, you should make sure that your school pack gives clear guidance about the system of rewards and sanctions used in your school. If you use a send-out system, please make sure you provide up-to-date information about where to send the pupil, and provide the necessary paperwork, such as send-out slips. If you use a detention system, please put detention slips in the supply teacher's pack and give details about how you arrange detention (e.g. who takes the detention, how long for, and when).

Whatever your system, if the supply teacher has to resort to sanctions, please, please back them up and make sure the sanction does take place. If not, it will be much harder for that teacher if faced with the same pupil again, and for any other supply teacher coming to the school. It is inevitable that if the sanction does not take place, some pupils will assume that they can get away with playing up in cover lessons.

Perhaps the single most useful tool in helping to maintain discipline is a class list. Taking a register at the start of the class can help to settle a class and identify pupils. Without this, the supply teacher either has to make their own list (which with some classes will end up full of Beckhams, Britneys and Bugs Bunnies), or do without a list, which can make it difficult if there is a need to report poor behaviour.

I have been to schools where class lists were not provided. At one I was told it was because it involved too much work. I did not go back.

Supply Teachers' Extras

The following is a bit of a wish list. I realise that not everything on the list is possible, or even necessary in every case, but these are a few things that could be useful in certain situations:

- a pigeon hole. I had one term-long contract where I would turn up to find rooms had been changed, computers were out of action, and classes had been cancelled – only to be told it was all in the newsletter, only I did not get one because I did not have a pigeon hole.

- a locker or somewhere to leave coats or bags. This is especially useful if the supply teacher is not attached to a particular department

- information about how to get photocopying done – and the code to be able to use the photocopier.

- access to a computer – and a password to be able to use it.

Cover Sheet

COVER SHEET			
Date	Period	Subject	Room No
Class Teacher		Class	
Lesson Title			
Aim/Learning Objectives			
Assessable Outcomes			
Source of Work Textbook Worksheets Video Computer Other			
Details			
Teaching Activity			
Starter			
Introduction			
Development			
Plenary			
Pupils with Special Needs			
Seating Plan			

Homework
         Task
 	
         Deadline			

Additional Notes			
Report on Class Behaviour (to be completed by cover teacher) Name Signature			

Supply Teachers' Handbook

The following is a suggested structure and contents list for a Supply Teacher's Handbook:

Please make sure the pages are numbered.

- Contents Page

- Welcome to the School
  - *a few words welcoming the teacher to the school*

- Daily Procedure for Supply Staff
  - *a clear description of what is expected of the supply teacher – e.g. Do they need to report to reception? Where will they find the cover co-ordinator? Do they need to wear a visitor's badge? Are they expected to attend staff briefings? What do they need to do at the end of the day? (e.g. sign out at reception, get timesheet signed).*

- School Timetable
  - *including times of breaks, assemblies, lessons (and whether or not bells are used to indicate start/end of lessons)*

- Registration
  - *a brief description, including where the registers are kept*

- Assembly
  - *a brief description of where and when, and any other helpful information*

- Cover Work
  - *where the cover work will be found*

- Sanctions and Rewards System
  - *including a brief description of accepted means of managing and rewarding pupil behaviour. Also include copies of necessary paperwork, e.g. send-out slips, referral slips, merits, credits etc.*

- Contact Names
  - *one or more contact names (and telephone extensions) for people who can be contacted for assistance with behavioural or medical issues*

- Health and Safety
  - *fire drills, medical emergencies*

- School Map
  - *a brief description of the school's layout and an up-to-date map or plan of the school*

- Other Information
  - *School Uniform*
  - *Classroom Etiquette*
  - *Toilets*
  - *Refreshments*
  - *Staff Room*
  - *Staff List*
  - *School History*

- Evaluation Form
  - *you may find it interesting to request feedback from your supply teachers.*

Insurance

Supply teachers should be covered by the school's Employers' Liability Insurance and Public Liability Insurance.

Employers' Liability Insurance

Employers are responsible for the health and safety of their employees while at work. Most employers are required by law to insure against liability for injury or disease to their employees arising out of their employment.

Employers' liability insurance is designed to enable employers to meet the cost of compensation for any employees' injuries or illness caused by their work while in your employment.

The Association of British Insurers (ABI) advises schools and local education authorities (LEAs) to make their insurers aware at the outset of any intention to use supply teachers, so that appropriate cover can be provided.

Public Liability Insurance

Public Liability Insurance provides cover for claims made against the school by members of the public or other businesses.

The ABI advises that a typical public liability policy will cover the consequences of acts undertaken by all teachers, whatever the nature of their employment status, whether permanent or temporary, part-time or full-time.

You may wish to clarify the situation with regard to both the above in relation to the employment of supply teachers by checking with the LEA or directly with the insurers.

Cover Supervisors

One of your options when looking at the management of cover for short-term absences in your school is to use cover supervisors.

What is a Cover Supervisor?

A cover supervisor is a member of a school's non-teaching or support staff who has the authority to look after a class of children. A cover supervisor is not the same as a Higher Level Teaching Assistant (HLTA), who could also look after a class of children, although an HLTA can become a cover supervisor.

The role of cover supervisor came about as a result of the Remodelling of the School Workforce reforms and the National Agreement on 'Raising Standards and Tackling Workload'.

What Can a Cover Supervisor Do?

A cover supervisor can supervise a class. Their role should be based around work that has been set by the class teacher. They should not be required to actively teach a class.

Typical aspects of a cover supervisor's work might be to read out the details of the work left for the pupils to do in class, manage the behaviour of the pupils, hand out any marked work, collect in work for marking, and report back on the behaviour of the pupils during the lesson.

Qualifications

There are no specific formal qualifications required to be a cover supervisor. Schools that request a certain level of qualification do so at their own discretion.

As the position involves working with children, an enhanced disclosure from the CRB would be required. Employers should also check that applicants have not been barred from working with children, by referring to the DfES List 99.

Cover supervisors need to have appropriate skills to manage class behaviour. Schools should facilitate appropriate training where needed.

Reasons to Use Cover Supervisors

Supporters of the use of cover supervisors and HLTAs to cover lessons argue that as they will be on a permanent contract with a school, their familiarity with the school's pupils, its ethos, and its policies and procedures will give them an advantage with classroom management that supply teachers who are new to the school would not have. The argument is that this will outweigh or at least balance the disadvantage of their lack of teaching qualifications or experience.

The financial reason to use cover supervisors is that they cost less per hour than a supply teacher. It will be for individual schools to balance the annual cost incurred by employing a cover supervisor on a permanent contract against the cost of employing a supply teacher only on days when needed.

THE SUPPLY AGENCY

What is a Supply Agency?

The Employment Agency Act 1973 defines an employment agency as being concerned with finding permanent work, and an employment business as dealing with temporary or contract positions. In reality, most people talk about employment agencies when referring to both permanent and temporary positions.

A supply agency is essentially an employment agency that specialises in placing teachers in schools on temporary contracts. These contracts could be one-off one-day bookings, regular weekly bookings throughout a whole term, or bookings covering longer absences such as maternity leave.

Supply agencies work with schools at all stages of education, including infant, junior, middle and secondary schools. They will also work with other education providers such as nurseries, special needs schools, Pupil Referral Units and Young Offenders Institutions.

Some supply agencies now also provide schools with cover supervisors on temporary contracts.

Although all supply agencies are employment agencies, not all employment agencies are supply agencies. Some prefer to focus on other markets, such as the commercial and industrial sectors, and avoid the education sector altogether.

Pros and Cons of Recruiting for the Education Sector

Some employment agencies operate solely as supply agencies, dealing only with the placement of teachers in schools to the exclusion of other areas of temporary employment. Other agencies prefer to avoid this sector completely.

This decision may be made due to the strength of local competition, the professional experience of the people setting up the agency, or the careful consideration of the pros and cons of working with the education sector. Some of these are outlined below.

Pros

With approximately 25,000 primary schools and 6,000 secondary schools in the United Kingdom, education is a major employer.

With the increasing pressures of work in schools and the change in the nature of teachers' work, long-term teacher absenteeism is growing.

The chargeable daily rate for teachers is higher than that in many other fields requiring temporary employment.

Cons

Teaching is effectively seasonal work, with a maximum of 39 weeks in a year in which there is a demand for teachers. Schools will usually close for two weeks at Christmas and Easter and six weeks during July and August. In addition, they will close for one-week half-term breaks in each of the three terms.

In addition to other supply agencies, you may also be competing with local education authorities (LEAs) which, in some areas, produce a register of teachers who are available as supply teachers. This register is made available to schools within the authority. As LEAs do not charge for this service, this method of booking supply teachers will usually be cheaper for schools than using agencies.

Because of the nature of the work, the agency is required by law to undertake more stringent checks before staff can be employed than in most other areas of work.

The insurance required for this sector is higher than in many other areas.

Recruitment and Employment Confederation (REC)

Having set up your agency, you might find it useful to become a member of the Recruitment and Employment Confederation (REC), which is a self-regulatory body representing the employment agency industry. It has an education division specifically catering for supply agencies.

The REC Education Sector Group has a Code of Practice that is binding on all its members. Agencies, schools and teachers can contact the REC in the case of a complaint or dispute.

One of the benefits of being a member of the REC is that once your agency has been trading for at least 12 months, you can apply for the REC Quality Mark, which was set up as a joint initiative between the Department for Education and Skills (DfES) and the REC.

The Quality Mark is awarded to supply agencies and LEAs that are deemed to meet specific standards of good practice in the supply and management of supply teachers to schools. Agencies that have been awarded the Quality Mark can use it to promote confidence in the quality of their service.

For further information, *see* page 143 or www.rec.co.uk.

Maintaining Standards

The supply of teachers to schools is a competitive market. The standard of service provided by your agency will be an important factor in attracting schools and teachers to use your services.

However successful your business may become, and however many schools and teachers you have on your books, it is important not to become complacent, as there are going to be many other agencies seeking to attract them away from you.

Agencies must always work to maintain a high standard of service and support to their clients and workers. At the very least, dissatisfaction could lead to schools and teachers changing agencies. More serious problems could lead to them complaining to the REC or to the Employment Agency Standards Inspectorate, which will investigate any complaints concerning agency conduct.

Even if you have maintained your standards, a failure to be aware of the competition and any new initiatives they may offer could lead to a loss of teachers and schools to other agencies.

Agencies must ensure that they keep up to date with developments in employment law. They are subject to routine inspections by the Employment Agency Standards Inspectorate, which is part of the Department of Trade and Industry (DTI), and which is specifically concerned with agencies' compliance with the law.

Agencies that have been awarded the REC Quality Mark can use this to illustrate that they meet standards of good practice in the provision and management of supply teachers to schools (*see* page 69 for further details).

Attracting Teachers to Your Agency

For a supply agency to succeed you must have good-quality teachers on your books.

If you are setting up a new agency, you will need to let teachers know who you are, where you are and what you offer that they would not be able to get from other agencies.

Most agencies place advertisements in local newspapers and in the main teachers' publication, *The Times Educational Supplement* (*TES*). Some advertisements give little more information than the agency name, telephone number and email address. Others provide a list of reasons why teachers should sign up with that agency rather than any other.

The basic question that your agency needs to be able to answer is: 'What makes you better than the rest?'

The majority of supply teachers will be looking for an agency that can offer them:

- a competitive rate of pay

- work when required, at schools they want to work at

- an accurate description of the schools where they are booked

- a professional service

- correct payment that reaches their account on time

- efficient handling and processing of paperwork

- supportive handling of any issues arising from schools

- friendly staff.

If you want to establish a good reputation among the local schools you must be prepared to turn teachers away if you do not feel confident in their ability to deliver a professional service. One bad experience with one of your teachers could be enough for a school to go elsewhere.

With every booking you must ensure that your teachers are properly briefed and aware of the nature of the school. This is particularly important when dealing with more challenging schools. You have a duty of care towards your supply teachers. Their understanding of the school will affect their ability to do a professional job. If they do not feel that you have been honest with them this could affect their willingness to work for your agency in the future.

Once you have established your agency you will need to keep building the number of teachers on your books. This can be achieved by further advertising and by incentives to teachers currently with you to recommend colleagues to your agency.

Checks on Supply Teachers

Once a prospective supply teacher has contacted you, you are required by law to undertake a number of checks before engaging them.

These are with regard to their identity, permission to work in the UK, qualifications, health and references. You must also ensure that they do not appear on the DfES List 99 of barred teachers.

In order to establish these, the supply teacher must be required to complete an application form, to submit the required documentation for you to verify, and to attend an interview.

The application form should seek information relating to personal circumstances, qualifications, teaching experience, employment history and medical history (*see* page 73 for an example).

The documentation, of which you must see the originals, should include:

- proof of identification (e.g. passport, birth certificate, or new-style driving licence)

- proof of address (e.g. utility bill or bank statement)

- recent passport photographs (at least two)

- a valid enhanced CRB disclosure certificate. If the teacher does not yet have one, they should complete a disclosure application form (teachers from overseas must have a notarised copy of an equivalent check from their home country)

- proof of qualifications, e.g. DfES letter or Certificate of Teaching Qualification (or equivalent in the case of overseas teachers. Consult the National Academic Recognition Information Centre (NARIC) list to see qualifications that are deemed equivalent)

- curriculum vitae (CV)

- references

- proof of registration with the General Teaching Council

- bank details.

The interview should enable you to gain an impression of the applicant's attitude towards work, their manner and their professionalism, and should help you to begin to build a rapport that will help your working relationship with them.

Sample Application Form

All documentation produced by the agency should be designed to reflect the image of the business and to ensure all legal requirements are addressed. The application form should cover the following:

APPLICATION FORM

Personal

Forename	Surname	Title
Address		
	Postcode	
Telephone	Email	
Date of Birth	Nationality	
National Insurance Number		

Teaching Preferences

Age Range Infant Junior Secondary Sixth form Other (please specify)				
Main Subject(s)	Other Subject(s)			
General Cover	Special Needs			
Days/Dates Available				
Geographical Area	Miles Prepared to Travel			

Employment History – Teaching

Dates	Organisation	Position

Employment History – Other

Dates	Organisation	Position

Teaching Qualifications/Experience

Teaching Qualifications	
Educational Establishment at which Qualified	
Year Qualified	Number of Years Teaching Experience

Qualifications

Qualifications	Level	Educational Establishment	Dates

Bank Details

Bank	Branch	Sort code	Account name and number

Legally Required

Applicants must be required to sign and date the application form, signifying their agreement to the following:

- I confirm that the information provided on this form is correct and complete.

- I confirm that I am legally entitled to work in the United Kingdom.

Teachers from Outside the United Kingdom

When taking on teachers who are not British citizens, it is the agency's responsibility to check that they have the right to work in the UK. It is, therefore, essential that the agency keeps abreast of any changes to the rules relating to this area, as these can have a significant impact on issues such as the nature of work, length of contract and length of stay in the UK.

It may also affect the documentation that you will need to check. Currently, in addition to that listed on page 72, you will need to see the originals, or certified copies, of the teacher's work permit or visa, passport, national police reference, medical certificate and qualifications. Where the teacher has qualified abroad, you will need to be confident that their teaching qualifications are equivalent to UK standards. If there is any doubt, contact the UK National Academic Recognition Information Centre (NARIC) on www.naric.org.uk.

Up-to-date information concerning teachers' eligibility to work in schools within the UK can be found at www.homeoffice.gov.uk; www.ukvisas.gov.uk; or www.workingintheuk.gov.uk.

A summary of the current situation is as follows:

EU Passport Holders

Supply teachers with British or EU passports can work in the UK without limitations.

European Economic Area (EEA)*

Supply teachers who are nationals of any country within the European Economic Area (EEA)* or Switzerland do not need permission to work in the UK and can be employed on the same basis as British teachers. Teachers from the Czech Republic, Estonia, Hungary, Latvia, Lithuania, Poland, Slovakia and Slovenia are required to register under the Worker Registration Scheme.

Commonwealth Teachers

Teachers from the Commonwealth can work as supply teachers on a working holidaymaker visa under certain circumstances. They must be 30 or under and without dependants. They must also be able to prove that they are mainly in the UK on holiday and that they are able to fund their holiday and their return without the need to work. They are not allowed to take contracts for more than four months, and are only allowed to work full-time for up to half of their holiday (up to a limit of one year of a two-year stay). Once the visa has expired, they are no longer allowed to continue to work in the UK.

Alternatively, a teacher from the Commonwealth may be working in the UK on a UK ancestry visa, which means they can work in the UK for up to five years.

Foreign Nationals

Teachers from other countries will need a work permit (unless they are coming to the UK under an approved exchange scheme, which is within the permit-free employment category).

Supply agencies are not eligible to apply for work permits on behalf of teachers. This has to be done by the school that is going to employ the teacher, and a permit will only be granted where there is a contract for at least four months. Once granted, the permit would enable the teacher to work at that school for up to four years.

The agency can be active in finding a school prepared to offer this level of work to a teacher, and in helping with the completion of paperwork, but it cannot apply for the work permit as an employer. Work permits will not be granted for casual or ad hoc supply work.

*EEA countries include: Austria, Belgium, Denmark, Finland, France, Germany, Greece, Iceland, Ireland, Italy, Liechtenstein, Luxembourg, the Netherlands, Norway, Portugal, Spain, Sweden and the United Kingdom.

Contract for Services

Once all the necessary checks have been completed to your satisfaction, you should provide each supply teacher with a written Contract for Services. This is similar in many ways to a Contract for Employment, which relates to permanent employment, but relates specifically to temporary work. It should set out the terms and conditions relating to the supply teacher's employment.

A Contract for Services:

- only applies to the days that the supply teacher works for the agency

- should make clear that the agency is there to offer work to the supply teacher

- should clarify that there is no obligation for the supply teacher to accept any offer

- should not seek to limit the supply teacher from signing up with other agencies.

A Contract for Services should protect both the teacher and the agency, ensuring that there are no surprises for either side.

Terms of Business

The Terms of Business relate to the contractual relationship between the agency and the school.

They should cover issues relating to charges, payment terms, and the implications should the nature of the teacher's employment provided by the agency change from temporary to permanent.

Schools should be required to confirm receipt and acceptance of the Terms of Business in writing. A signed copy of the Terms of Business returned to the agency is generally accepted for this purpose.

Teachers' Pay

The system and level of pay that you offer to your teachers is likely to be a significant factor in a teacher's decision to sign up with your agency or one of your competitors. For this reason your system needs to be clear and easily comparable.

Your rates must be competitive. If you do not offer the highest rates then you must offer other benefits that teachers will consider enough of an incentive to compensate for accepting a lower rate of pay, for example a higher amount of work than they might expect to get from other agencies.

Teachers will want to know how their pay will be calculated. The two main systems appear to be either to calculate pay in relation to the teachers' pay spine, or to offer a flat rate, with slight variations relating to certain circumstances, e.g. higher rates for long-term bookings, for teachers prepared to travel further, or for those who are prepared to go to less 'popular' schools.

Teachers will also look at whether they are to be paid weekly or monthly, and whether or not they can claim holiday pay during school holidays.

They may also want to know whether there will be financial implications if a school offers them a permanent contract.

The agency is responsible for paying the supply teacher and, where appropriate, for the deduction and payment of National Insurance contributions and Pay As You Earn (PAYE) income tax.

The legal rights and responsibilities of each party are laid out in the Income Tax (Earnings and Pensions) Act 2003.

The agency is also responsible for issuing P60s to all supply staff at the financial year-end and a P45 at the end of employment.

Information to Give to Supply Teachers

As soon as the necessary checks have been undertaken and a Contract for Services signed, you can start to send the teacher out on bookings.

The quality of the work undertaken by the teacher will reflect on your agency and will affect the school's willingness to use your agency in future. It is therefore important to try to ensure that there is a good match between the school and the teacher.

As the teacher is not obliged to take any booking, it may be tempting to try to make the school sound more appealing than it is. However, this could have serious implications for your business. If the teacher is unable to cope at the school they may not be prepared to work for you again, and if the school is unhappy with the teacher's performance they may not use your agency again.

The best approach is to provide as accurate a picture as you can, and approach the teachers you believe to be best suited to individual bookings, because of subject specialism, age specialism or behaviour-management skills.

The amount of information you are able to provide will depend to a certain extent on whether this is a last-minute booking or one with plenty of notice. The essentials are:

- clear directions – and a map, if possible

- contact number for the school

- the name of the person responsible for organising supply cover at the school

- the time the supply teacher should arrive at the school

- details of cover – e.g. age range and subject (if known)

- some idea of the nature of the school

- plenty of timesheets to complete (if used by the agency)

- any additional information that will help the supply teacher do their job well.

Some of the information packs provided by schools are sadly lacking. They can range from two sides of A4 to 40-page books. More is not always better. I have found that some of the tomes I have been handed have been full of largely irrelevant information. And perhaps because of their length and the amount of work involved in producing them, they seem more likely to be out of date.

Depending on your relationship with the school and the number of teachers you place there for supply, you may find it benefits everyone to provide the school with a checklist of helpful information to put together into a basic handbook of information. You can then have copies to send to your teachers.

Timesheets

Most agencies require their supply teachers to submit timesheets as proof of work completed.

These timesheets should be completed at the end of any assignment lasting less than a week, or on a weekly basis for longer-term contracts.

As with any documentation, it is useful to design your timesheets to reflect the style and work of your business. On a practical level, they should also be photocopiable and faxable.

You may wish to consider producing timesheets with pre-printed carbon copies to give to each of the parties involved: agency, client and contractor.

When designing a new timesheet, you will probably want to include the company logo, name and address, telephone number, and email and website addresses. If it is acceptable for teachers to fax in completed timesheets, then also include the fax number.

Make sure the instructions are clear, emphasise the need to submit the timesheet as soon as possible, and give a deadline day if appropriate.

The main part of the timesheet should provide space for the supply teacher to complete the necessary information to make their claim. This will include:

- school name

- school address

- number of hours or days worked

- dates of days worked

- date of submission of form

- name of supply teacher

- signature of supply teacher

- name and position of authorised representative of school

- signature of authorised representative of school.

You may also wish to add a statement to the effect that by signing the timesheet the client agrees to the Terms of Business (*see* page 75).

Supporting Your Supply Teachers

Working as a supply teacher can be a lonely business. If there is not much work around, or it tends to consist of only one or two days in a school, there is not much opportunity to build up a rapport with other teachers. As a result, contact with the agency becomes more important, even a lifeline.

I have been lucky to find agencies that are friendly, and I have really appreciated the social events that have been arranged for their supply teachers. Little touches like a card at Christmas and on my birthday have also been much appreciated.

Passing on positive feedback is also to be recommended. Knowing that a school has specifically asked for you, or finding out that your name has been mentioned in the school's evaluation form, is good to know and helps maintain motivation.

Dealing with Problems

Even when you have met your legal responsibility to make sure that your teachers are qualified, experienced and legally entitled to work in the United Kingdom, this does not guarantee that they will do a good job.

If a teacher or school complains, or if you think for any reason a teacher is having or causing problems, you must take immediate action.

Schools that are unhappy with your teachers are unlikely to use your services again unless they are satisfied with the way that you have dealt with the problem, and teachers who are unhappy with the school(s) that you are sending them to may also be unwilling to work for you again.

The first course of action should be to talk to the school and to the teacher to find out what the problem is. You should also consider your own part in the situation. For example, was the teacher properly briefed? Would this have affected the issue in any way?

The next step will depend on the nature of the complaint. An issue such as turning up late would obviously require different action to an inability to manage the children, swearing or hitting a child.

If it appears that the school is being unreasonable, you should be prepared to support the teacher. Bear in mind there are two sides to every story. You may need to adopt the role of an arbitrator to help the school and the teacher reach an agreement. You will need to make an informed decision as to the action you may wish to take. The ideal situation is to keep the school as a client and the supply teacher as a contractor.

Whatever your solution, you must write to the school outlining your course of action as soon as possible. The Recruitment and Employment Confederation (REC) recommends that this should be within two days.

Attracting Schools to Your Agency

To be successful you need to convince the schools in your area that it is to their advantage to use your agency rather than the local education authority (LEA) register, their own pool of teachers, or another agency.

The first step is to make sure the schools know about your agency, what services you provide, where you are, and how to contact you. The best way to do this is by a combination of phone calls, direct mail and visits to the schools. Getting through to teaching staff by phone is always difficult, but if nothing else a phone call should get you a contact name. Whether you are contacting the school by phone or letter, the aim should be to arrange a meeting at the school.

Most people find it easier to deal with people they have met, so arranging a meeting to visit the cover co-ordinator is a good idea. In addition, if you have visited the school, met some of the staff and seen the pupils, you are going to have a better idea of the nature and ethos of the school, which hopefully will help you select the best person for the job and brief them appropriately.

The hardest step is to convince schools to try your services for the first time. This will be even harder if the school is happy with its current system. The best you may be able to hope for is to persuade the school to use you as a back-up. This means that your first booking with the school is likely to be either at very short notice or for a shortage area where few subject specialists are available, and where other agencies have failed.

Once you have successfully got your first booking, it is up to you to make sure you place the best teacher you can and provide the best service you can to encourage the school to use you again.

The ideal scenario for any agency is to be a school's agency of choice, the one that the school automatically contacts to provide teachers. Achieving this will depend to an extent on the strength of the competition, but factors that will help will include the quality of the teachers provided, the cost, the ability to meet the school's needs at short notice and the professionalism of the agency.

Some agencies will offer schools preferential terms if they enter into a sole-supplier agreement or a preferred-supplier agreement.

Even if you have not provided a school with supply teachers for a while, it is a good idea to maintain regular contact with them. At the same time it is important to remember the time constraints on teaching staff: they will not want to be bothered by needless telephone calls. So, sending out regular newsletters or résumés, which you think may be of interest to a school, may be a better alternative.

What a School Expects from a Supply Agency

Schools will be looking for certain qualities from their agencies. These are likely to include:

- ***Well-qualified, professional teachers***

It is the agency's legal responsibility to ensure they obtain enough information from schools to be able to identify suitable teachers for positions. Schools must be able to rely on the agency to send qualified teachers, with a professional and responsible attitude towards their pupils and their work, who will turn up on time and be dressed appropriately. If this is not the case, the schools will soon start to use other agencies. An agency is only as good as the teachers it sends into schools.

- ***Ability to provide appropriate supply teachers as and when required***

Bookings are often made at very short notice, so do not be surprised if you get a call at 8.15 a.m. from a school wanting a teacher to cover the first lesson, which is starting at 8.40 a.m. If you are lucky you will have a teacher on your books who lives around the corner from the school, who is available, and who has the required subject specialism.

If not, you may yet be able to save the day. All you need is a good supply teacher who can get to the school in reasonable time. Most schools will accept that at such short notice the likelihood of someone getting to them in time for the first lesson is slight. So, as long as you are honest with them about the time your supply teacher will arrive, most schools will be happy to know someone is on their way.

- ***Competitive rates***

Cost is always going to be an issue. Schools on tight budgets will be concerned to ensure they get value for money when making arrangements for cover. At the same time, however, they have an obligation to provide an effective learning environment for their pupils. In the same way that some teachers will look for the agency that is able to pay them the most, some schools will be tempted to use the agency that will charge them the least. This is fine so long as that agency also provides good-quality teachers and a professional service. If the local education authority (LEA) provides a register of supply teachers, the agency is unlikely to be able to compete on cost, so it must rely on other factors to encourage schools to use its services.

- ***A professional service***

Schools will expect to receive appropriate information from the agency about the teachers booked, to be invoiced promptly, and for any issues arising to be dealt with professionally. They may look at accreditations held by the agency as an indication of the quality of service that can be expected, for example looking at International Standards Organisation (ISO), Investors in People (IIP) and Recruitment and Employment Confederation (REC) awards.

- ***Efficient handling of any issues***

Schools will need to be confident that any complaints will be dealt with promptly and efficiently and that the school will be kept informed of any action taken.

- ***Awareness and adherence to legal requirements***

Schools must be able to rely on their supply agency to undertake thorough checks of all the teachers on its books, including ensuring that all teachers have an up-to-date Criminal Records Bureau (CRB) enhanced disclosure, are suitably qualified and entitled to work in the UK, and by following up all references. Some schools may require a list of the checks undertaken and a written assurance that these have been completed.

Information to Give to Schools

The basic information a school will expect regarding any supply teacher will be the teacher's name, a brief outline of their experience and, unless required for general cover, their subject specialism. Always ensure that the information you provide to the school about your teachers is clear and accurate.

A school should be able to take it for granted that the agency has undertaken all the necessary checks regarding the teacher's identity, qualifications, references, criminal record, permission to work and health. Some may require a written assurance to this effect. If for any reason it was found that you had failed in this duty, it is unlikely that a school would ever trust you to supply them with staff again.

Some schools also like to receive a photograph. However, as the only one I have ever seen of myself had been faxed through and I looked like someone with dark hair, beard and moustache (I am female with fair hair and definitely clean shaven), I didn't think this was particularly helpful.

In addition, it is always a good idea to ring the school on the first day of the booking to ensure that the teacher has arrived safely and on time.

If it is your first booking with the school it is also recommended that you ring at the end of the day to ensure that the school was satisfied with the service provided or to send a feedback form for the school to complete. An example of such a form can be found on page 84.

Feedback Form

The following example of a feedback form shows a possible layout and outlines the type of information that you could seek. The key is to ensure that it is not too long or complicated, but does cover the main areas of interest.

FEEDBACK FORM

As we pride ourselves on the quality of service that we and our teachers provide, and are constantly striving to find ways to improve, we would be grateful if you could complete and return this feedback form in the stamped addressed envelope provided.

Name of supply teacher ....

Date of employment   from ....   to ....

Please indicate your view of the teacher by ticking the appropriate boxes.

	Excellent	Very Good	Good	Average	Poor
Attitude to work	☐	☐	☐	☐	☐
Professionalism	☐	☐	☐	☐	☐
Time-keeping	☐	☐	☐	☐	☐
Appearance	☐	☐	☐	☐	☐

Would you re-employ them?   Yes ☐   No ☐

If no, please give reasons ....

Any other comments ....

....

Please indicate your opinion of the agency by ticking the most appropriate boxes.

	Excellent	Very Good	Good	Average	Poor
Efficiency	☐	☐	☐	☐	☐
Attitude	☐	☐	☐	☐	☐
Reliability	☐	☐	☐	☐	☐
Communication	☐	☐	☐	☐	☐
Finance	☐	☐	☐	☐	☐
Overall quality	☐	☐	☐	☐	☐

Any other comments ....

....

Name ....   Signature ....

School ....   Position...

Postcode ....   Date ....

Thank you for your time in providing this feedback.

Charges

The charges to the school will mainly comprise the supply teacher's pay. There will also be the employer's National Insurance contributions (NIC), holiday pay and any expenses that may be agreed. In addition, there will be the agency's margin, which is usually calculated as a percentage of the supply teacher's pay. VAT, if applicable, will be payable on the entirety of the charges.

Charges to the school = teacher's pay + holiday-pay provision + employer's NIC + agency's profit margin.

The charges will be invoiced to the schools on a weekly basis, and are payable within seven days, or as stated in the Terms of Business.

As with other businesses, agencies are entitled to charge interest on any overdue amounts at 4 per cent above the base rate from the due date until the date of payment.

Permanent Contracts

As one of an agency's aims is to ensure a good match between its teachers and schools, the offer of a permanent contract to one of its supply teachers from one of its schools should be seen as a good thing, because it shows it has got it right. However, this also represents a loss of income, as the teacher will no longer be available for supply. As a result, agencies will usually have a policy for dealing with this situation.

The policy concerning the engagement of supply teachers on permanent contracts will vary between agencies and should be clearly stated in the agency's Terms of Business (*see* page 75).

Some agencies will require a supply teacher to be kept on a temporary contract for a given period before being taken on to a permanent contract. Others will require a transfer fee, which may vary depending on the time the supply teacher has been at a school before going on to a permanent contract, and whether or not the contract is for a fixed term. Some agencies are happy to waive fees if the teacher has already been at the school for a given period.

If the parties involved negotiate an alternative agreement, they should ensure that any variations to the Terms of Business are made in writing in order to avoid any confusion or dispute that could arise at a later date.

The Law

Supply agencies, as with other employment agencies, must adhere to the regulations set out by the Employment Agency Act 1973, and the Conduct of Employment Agencies and Employment Businesses Regulations 2003. These lay out the legal rights and responsibilities of each of the parties involved: the client (school), agency and contractor (supply teacher).

Agencies should also ensure that their staff are fully aware of, and comply with, the child protection provisions of the Criminal Justice and Court Services Act 2000, the Education Reform Act 1988, the Protection of Children Act 1999, the Care Standards Act 2000, and the Education (Restriction of Employment) Regulations 2000.

It Is the responsibility ot the supply agency to obtain sufficient information from the school to enable it to provide the school with an appropriate teacher: for example, the dates and duration of the work, the type of work and whether any special qualifications or experience are required.

Once this has been established, it is the agency's legal responsibility to confirm the supply teacher's eligibility to work in the UK and in schools, also their identity, qualifications, experience and training. This includes applying for a CRB enhanced disclosure (*see* page 88), obtaining copies of any relevant qualifications and obtaining at least two references. Copies should be made available to the school if requested.

The legal relationship of the agency and supply teacher is that of employer and employee. As the work is temporary, supply agencies are required to provide a Contract for Services for each supply teacher which should outline the terms and conditions of their employment (*see* page 75 for further details).

The supply agency will also have a contract with the schools for which it is providing teachers. The terms of this contract (known as the Terms of Business) will need to be agreed between the parties. It is in the interests of the agency to ensure issues such as notice required for cancelled bookings, risk assessments, treatment of staff while on the school premises and procedures in the case of unsatisfactory staff are covered (*see* page 75).

It is vital that agencies are aware that the law relating to employment is continually evolving, and that they keep abreast of changes to the law. This applies to both British and European law. For example, the EU Working Time Directive 2003 lays down provisions for a maximum 48-hour working week (including overtime), rest periods and breaks and a minimum of four weeks paid leave per year. It applies to both public and private sectors, and permanent and temporary employment. Supply teachers are therefore entitled to claim for paid holiday.

If your agency is a member of the Recruitment and Employment Confederation (REC) it can access a range of legal services available on all aspects of recruitment law (*see* www.rec.co.uk for further information).

Criminal Records Bureau (CRB) Disclosure Requirements

Because of the nature of the work, the post of supply teacher is exempt from the provisions of section 4 of the Rehabilitation of Offenders Act 1974. This means that applicants are not entitled to withhold information about convictions that would otherwise be regarded as 'spent' under the provisions of the Act.

As a result, supply teachers must have an enhanced disclosure certificate from the Criminal Records Bureau. This can be arranged by, and at the expense of, the agency, or by the teachers themselves.

An enhanced disclosure contains the following information:

- details of convictions, including those 'spent' under the Rehabilitation of Offenders Act 1974

- cautions held at national level

- information from local police records, including relevant non-conviction information

- whether the individual is included on any of the following lists: List 99, POCAL (Protection of Children Act List), or the Scottish equivalent, the Protection of Children (Scotland) Act.

CRB certificates are not transferable between agencies. This means that an agency is required, by law, to apply for a CRB check for every teacher on its books, even if a teacher already has a valid CRB certificate from another agency.

The information contained in the disclosure is derived from police records, and from records of people who have been identified as being unsuitable to work with children. The CRB uses the Police National Computer, which contains details of convictions, cautions, reprimands and final warnings in England and Wales, and most of the relevant convictions in Scotland.

With this and other checks, the agency must see the originals and keep copies.

Government Department Lists

Agencies are required by law to check the Department for Education and Skills (DfES) List 99 and the Department of Health (DoH) Protection of Children Act List (POCAL), or the Scottish equivalent, before employing supply teachers. This is undertaken as part of the Criminal Records Bureau (CRB) enhanced disclosure check (*see* page 88).

These lists contain the names, dates of birth and teacher-reference numbers of people who are partly or completely barred from teaching children.

Their names could be on the list on grounds of misconduct or for medical reasons. Their employment could be barred or restricted. If restricted, types of permitted employment will be identified.

Copies of List 99 are usually held by the local education authority (LEA), further-education organisations and associations representing independent schools. If the agency does not have access to the latest list, it can write to the DfES quoting the teacher's full name, date of birth and, if they have one, their DfES reference number. Urgent requests can be made by fax.

Where a teacher is not used continuously, the agency should repeat the check annually.

It is unlawful to employ anyone in a post from which they are barred. If it is found that the teacher is not totally barred, but is subject to restrictions on their employment, under no circumstances should they be placed in a post that would in any way infringe those restrictions. If such a teacher is supplied to a school, the agency must tell the head teacher of the restrictions imposed on that person's employment.

More information on this can be found in DfES Circular 11/95: Misconduct of Teachers and Workers with Children and Young Persons and in *The Protection of Children Act 1999: A Practical Guide to the Act for all Organisations Working with Children*.

EMERGENCY ACTIVITIES

FOR

COVER LESSONS

Emergency Activities

One of the worst things that can happen to a cover teacher is that you arrive at the classroom, the pupils are already there waiting for you to start, and there is no sign of any work. At this point you do not know whether anyone is going to turn up with some work or if you are going to have to improvise for the whole lesson.

All the time you are waiting, the class is getting unsettled. Even if work does arrive, by this time you may well have lost the attention of the class.

After being faced with this situation on several occasions, I put together a bank of activities that I could use either as introductory ice-breakers, settlers, or for whole lessons.

Even if cover work has been set, I find it useful to give the class a five-minute activity to tackle straight away so the pupils are occupied while I familiarise myself with the work or while I am being briefed.

Most supply teachers build up their own stock of resources and activities that they can use in an emergency. You will find a pocket on the inside of the back cover where these can be kept.

If, however, you need a new activity, you will find plenty of ideas in the following pages, for a wide range of subjects, for primary and secondary pupils.

As you are usually already in the classroom with your pupils before you find out that no work has been left, the main criteria for the following activities is that they do not require photocopying or any equipment other than what would normally be found in a typical classroom – i.e. paper and pens.

Each of the activities has been written so that it can be given as it is to the class.

Alternatively, you might wish to adapt it to suit the age and ability level of the class, or to suit your own preferences and level of expertise.

Possible adaptations are suggested in italics.

When I am in the situation where I need to find a suitable activity, I try to find out as much as I can about the work the pupils have being doing in previous lessons and set an activity related to this. Pupils can generally tell when they have been given a time-filler and when their activity is educational. Their behaviour often reflects their opinion, so it is worth that extra bit of effort.

General Activities

The following activities can be adapted for all ages and all subjects.

Hangman

Pupils can take turns to draw a number of short lines representing the letters in a mystery word or phrase on the board. The other pupils suggest letters or guess at the total word or phrase. The words or phrases must relate to the subject being covered.

If they correctly guess a letter it is written in the right place on the board. Any incorrect guess results in a part of the hangman picture being drawn. If the drawing is completed the class has lost.

You can set all the words, or you could just set the first one, so that the pupils are clear about the rules. After this, the pupil who guesses the answer first can set the next one.

This works best with smaller groups. It could get out of hand with too large a group.

Quizzes

Each pupil, or pupils working in groups, can be asked to set a given number of quiz questions. They must, of course, know the answers to the questions they have set. You may also want to set some of your own questions.

All the questions must relate to the subject being covered.

All the contributions are then written on the board for the class to answer.

A prize can be offered to the pupil, or team, who gets the most questions right.

Crosswords

Pupils can be asked to design crosswords in almost any subject. It can be a good test of their knowledge and understanding of the subject and they usually enjoy the challenge of designing a crossword that will beat their fellow pupils.

If you know beforehand that you are going to have a class with no set work, you might like to create your own crossword.

A useful website to help with this is www.eclipsecrossword.com.

Word Searches

A word search involves pupils thinking about words relevant to the subject being studied and hiding them in a grid of letters.

With younger or lower-ability groups, you may prefer to provide pupils with a list of words. You may also find it useful to specify the size of the grid.

For older and more able pupils, the activity can be made more interesting by asking them to write clues that have to be solved in order to find out which words are hidden in the grid.

Once the pupils have completed their word searches, they can swap them with another pupil to solve.

Primary School Activities

ART AND DESIGN

Activity One
I will read out a description of something that I would like you to draw. You will need to listen very carefully and to draw as I speak.

Draw something on a piece of paper. It can be something familiar, such as a car or a boat, or a series of shapes, letters and numbers, which you then describe to the pupils. This is a good activity for developing listening skills and the pupils usually enjoy seeing the varied results. It is also a good activity for practising use of directional language such as above, below, left, right, and comparative language such as bigger, smaller etc.

The pupil with the best interpretation can then be asked to draw a picture and to describe it to the class, or this can be organised in small groups.

Activity Two
Draw a picture of one of your friends in the class.

You may prefer to give each pupil the name of someone else in the class so that everyone gets a picture of themselves.

This activity can be introduced by asking pupils to describe themselves (or each other). What do they consider to be their main features? Encourage them to think about how they would show something about their personality in their picture, e.g. by adding a toy or pet, by what they are wearing or their pose.

The activity can be concluded by asking the pupils to guess who the person is in each picture.

Activity Three
Draw a picture of the weather.

You could specify the type of weather, for example a sunny day, a wet and/or windy day, or you could add a twist, for example a storm in a teacup, or relate it to a nursery rhyme or favourite story.

This activity could be developed to include a poem about the weather, or a descriptive piece of writing.

Activity Four
What is a chair? Why do we use them? Think of as many different types of chair as you can.

Suggested chairs might include a throne, deckchair, kitchen chair, lounge chair, computer chair.

Once the pupils have suggested a number of chairs, organise them into groups and encourage them to look carefully at a chair. Name its different parts. Do all chairs have the same parts? What aspects of the chair could change? e.g. materials, size, construction.

Design a chair for a specific character, e.g. a character from a nursery rhyme, short story or favourite story.

Activity Five
Make a picture of the season.

This could be a collage or painting, bringing together images relating to a specific season.

If computers are available pupils could use a drawing package to show the different seasons.

Useful Websites
See page 139.

DESIGN AND TECHNOLOGY (D&T)

Activity One
Make a list of as many different foods as you can think of. Try to think of one for each letter of the alphabet. Draw a picture of each one. Cut out your pictures. Put the foods into groups, e.g. fruit, vegetables, meat, fish, and dairy products.

Possibilities include apple, beetroot, cucumber, doughnut, egg, fish, grape, haddock, ice cream, jelly, kebab, lemon, milk, nut, orange, pineapple, quiche, rice, strawberry, tomato, Ugli fruit, vinegar, waffle, xanthan gum (a thickener in ice cream and dairy products), yoghurt, zabaglione.

Activity Two
Design a menu describing the meal you are going to eat for lunch. Do you know what the ingredients are? List as many as you can.

Activity Three
You have made a new-flavour crisp. What flavour is it? What is it going to be called? What will the packet look like? What colour will it be? What information do you need to write on the packet?

Activity Four
Design a container from a single piece of paper to hold something fragile or precious, e.g. Cinderella's slipper, the Queen's jewels.

A good way to introduce this is to start by asking the pupils to think of as many containers as they can, and to write them down in a list. Encourage them to think about the different materials they are made from. Examples might include a jewellery box, a safe or a cat basket. This can also be linked to examples in nature, such as egg shells, birds' nests, a kangaroo's pouch etc.

Activity Five
Design an item of clothing for a character from a nursery rhyme, song or story.

The context for this activity can be set by reading a short story, a nursery rhyme or relating it to a well-known story. For example, designing a cloak for Little Red Riding Hood or an outfit for a wizard.

Activity Six
Write a list of five things that you can see in the room. Now list them in alphabetical order. Write a description of each one. What is it used for? What is it made from? Why do you think this material was used? Can you think of another material that could be used instead? Would it be as good? Why/Why not?

This activity can be made easier using a template of four boxes drawn on an A4 sheet with the headings: What is it? What is it for? What is it made from? Why? You might want to give an example to help the pupils, e.g. it is a window. It is used to look through and to let light in. It is made from glass. We can see through it (it is transparent).

This activity can be extended by also asking pupils to think about other materials that could be used instead and to give reasons why these would be better or not so good.

Activity Seven
Your challenge is to build a bridge using the materials provided.

This activity can be varied by specifying a distance that the bridge has to span, e.g. 50 cm, or a weight it must be able to support, e.g. 50g, or the challenge can be to build the tallest tower. The only materials needed are paper (newspaper or A4), paper clips and sticky tape. This activity can be linked to Science.

You may wish to organise pupils into teams to undertake this activity.

Useful Websites
See page 139.

96

ENGLISH

Activity One

This is the first time I have met you, and I would really like to get to know you, so I would like you to write me a letter telling me all about yourself. I would like you to start by telling me what you are like, for example are you naughty or well-behaved? What do you like doing? Do you like playing games? Are you noisy or quiet?

Pupils who finish quickly can add a description about what they look like. At the end you could read out the letters and see if the class can guess who they are from. An alternative for younger pupils would be to produce a drawing, supported by simple sentences, describing themselves.

Activity Two

Listen to my story. When I have finished you are going to write your own stories.

Pupils could be asked to retell your story, to make up their own, or to write a story about themselves. They could tell the story using pictures only, or pictures and writing, depending on their ability, and recorded in a zig-zag book (cut a piece of A3 paper in half lengthways, and fold up into a concertina).

Activity Three

Write an article for the school magazine, e.g. 'New Teacher Arrives in School'.

This could be developed as part of the next activity.

Activity Four

We are going to make a newspaper/school magazine. We are going to start by thinking about all the different things people might be interested in reading about. In order to do this we need to give out some jobs, for example News Editor, Health and Beauty Editor, Sports Editor.

It is helpful if you have some newspapers and magazines for pupils to look through to see the sort of information they could put in. They might add a food section, travel, cars, advertising, agony aunt and TV listings. Working in small groups, they can then each write an article to be included in their section.

Activity Five

When I arrived at school I was the only person here. Where was everyone? What had happened to them? Had I come to the right place? Was it the right day? What could I do? What would you do if you came to school and couldn't find anyone? Write a short story about the day you arrived at school and no one else was there.

Other possible titles include: 'A Mysterious Teacher Arrives in School'; or 'The Day the Lights Went Out'.

Activity Six

Write a short poem about yourself.

Other possible themes include the school, the sea, the seasons, a holiday or a famous person. Younger pupils may need a writing frame and examples to help them.

Activity Seven

Make a classroom display of the letters of the alphabet.

If you have newspapers and magazines available, ask the pupils to cut out all the examples they can find of a letter in as many different styles as they can, including capitals and italics, and use these to make a large display version of that letter. You may find it helpful to cut out a large shape of a letter to use as a base.

This could be organised so that each child is working on one letter (plus !s and ?s if needed) or you could organise the pupils into groups, for example working on the vowels.

Useful Websites

See page 139.

Geography

Activity One
Can you remember your first day at school? How did you find your way around? I go to lots of schools and they are all different, so I could really do with some help. I would like you to draw me a map of the school so that I can find my way around.

This can be linked to literacy by asking pupils to write directions to each of the places identified.

Activity Two
I think this is a lovely place to live because I like to *(climb mountains, go to the coast, go shopping, etc)*. What do you think is the best thing about living here?

I think we should make a leaflet/advertisement telling other people everything we like about 'here'.

If you have access to computers it is helpful if you can download local information or pictures.

Activity Three
Today's date is (say a date in a different season). This means we are in which season? What sort of weather do we get? Draw a picture to show the weather in each season.

Older and more able pupils could be asked to write a description to go with their picture. If computers are available pupils could use a drawing package to illustrate the seasons.

Activity Four
Today we are going to go on a trip abroad. How many of you have your passports with you? If you haven't got one, we'll have to make one.

A passport can be simply made using a single sheet of A4 folded in half. Pupils should write passport on the front and decorate. On the top half of the inside front page they can draw a picture of themselves, or stick in a photograph of themselves if digital cameras are available. Underneath they should write their name, date of birth and place of birth. The third page is then available for stamps for the countries they have visited.

This activity can be linked with Activity Five and with Design and Technology.

Activity Five
Who would like to go on a trip abroad? Where shall we go? Let's choose a country. Why do we want to go there? What do we know about it?

It works quite well if the pupils have different suggestions about where they want to go, as they can be put into groups with the task of finding out as much as they can about their chosen country. They then have to make their case to the others as to why their idea is the best. The information can be presented in a leaflet, as a poster or by pupils standing up and telling the others.

This can be linked to drama and literacy. Tell the pupils to imagine they are on a magic carpet and ask them questions such as: Where are we going? How does it feel? What can you see?

Activity Six
Who likes going on holiday? Where do you like to go? What do you like to do on holiday?

I would like to know more about your holidays, so I would like you to design a questionnaire to find out about people's holidays.

Pupils should be encouraged to ask questions that will help them find out where people have been, what they enjoy about holidays, and where they would like to go in the future. Once the questionnaires have been designed, the pupils can ask each other the questions. This activity links to Mathematics, as the results can be recorded using tallies, tables, charts and graphs.

Useful Websites
See page 139.

HISTORY

Activity One
Draw a timeline of your life.

Significant dates could be illustrated in an appropriate way, e.g. picture of baby to illustrate their birth or the arrival of a sibling, and a school for their first day at school.

This could be developed by asking pupils to project into the future, e.g. a car when they think they will pass their driving test.

An alternative is to draw a timeline of their day. It can be very detailed: have breakfast, clean teeth, brush hair, go to school, go to bed etc.

Activity Two
Think about how life has changed in recent times.

This activity could be made more specific by focusing on school days, toys, food, clothes or holidays. You may need to help pupils by telling them about your memories of when you were a child, or by using a story to describe what life was like further back in time.

Activity Three
Who likes holidays? Why do we have holidays? When do we have holidays?

Encourage the pupils to name all the holidays we have in a year. Once you have a reasonable list, you can ask the pupils to put them in date order. This can be developed into a timeline, showing when each holiday occurs in a year. Pupils can then be asked to write a description or draw pictures describing what is important about each holiday and what we do during each holiday.

This could also be linked to a discussion about the history of each holiday, and their links with religious festivals.

Activity Four
Draw a picture of the outside of your home. Label the main features, e.g. the windows, door, walls and roof.

This can lead to a discussion about the different types of places that people live in, e.g. bungalows, houses and flats. Encourage pupils to think about more unusual examples, e.g. houseboats and caravans. Talk about where people lived in different times in the past, e.g. caves, huts, forts, Roman villas.

This activity can involve pupils in drawing pictures of homes through history, labelling the different parts and listing the different materials used. They could also draw a timeline, showing the development of homes through time.

Activity Five
Describe what you are wearing. Do you have a favourite thing to wear? What do you like about it? Is it the colour, the material, or something else?

Have people always worn the same clothes as you are wearing? What did people wear in the Stone Age, or Roman times, or Victorian times?

If the pupils have been studying a particular period, you could focus on this for comparison or, if you have books or computers available you can encourage them to do some research and draw pictures showing the different types of clothes, and describe the different materials and colours that would be worn.

Younger pupils will need pictures to support them in this activity.

Useful Websites
See page 139.

INFORMATION AND COMMUNICATION TECHNOLOGY (ICT)

Activity One
Write a list of what we use computers for, e.g. writing, calculations, drawing, computer control. Have we always used computers? How did we do these things in the past?

You may need to prompt pupils to think about what they use computers for, e.g. writing, calculations, drawing, computer control, games, listening to music, learning etc.

If you have access to computers, and if the school's policy allows the use of the internet for research, pupils could search for information and pictures relating to the history of these functions, e.g. pictures of quills and old-fashioned typewriters.

Activity Two
Draw a picture of a computer. Label all the different parts.

The pupils may need to be prompted to include keyboard, monitor, CPU (central processing unit), mouse, floppy disk, CD-ROM.

Activity Three
Find out the meaning of these words: computer, mouse, keyboard, computer monitor, floppy disk, hard drive.

You can add to the suggested list or replace them with words related to the work the pupils are doing. The pupils can find out the meanings of words using Google (type in define:computer and a number of definitions will appear. There should not be any spaces either side of the colon). Alternatively, use online dictionaries such as www.factmonster.com or www.wordcentral.com (check the school policy regarding the use of the internet first).

Activity Four
Log on to www.bbc.co.uk/schools. Click on 'other subjects'.

There are a number of very useful sites on the internet that offer information, activities and games relating to a number of subjects, including ICT. At the time of writing, the BBC site had a useful activity for familiarising pupils with the computer keyboard.

Activity Five
Make a poster about your school. Make sure you include pictures, the name and address of the school and the school logo.

This activity can be adapted to focus on one of the subjects studied in school, or it can be about the school as a whole. Pupils should be encouraged to experiment with layout of text and pictures, using one or more computer packages.

An alternative would be for pupils to make a leaflet about the school.

Activity Six
You are going to put together a school magazine. You are going to write the articles, take the pictures and put it all together into the different sections. The first thing to do is to decide what sort of information you are going to include. What do you like to read about in magazines and comics? How big do you think the magazine should be? How many different sections should you include?

When discussing what the magazine will look like, it would be helpful to have some examples. Encourage pupils to look at the fonts that are used, the headings, and the way the articles are laid out on the page.

The easiest way to manage this activity is to put pupils into small groups, each working on a different area, e.g. news, health and beauty, sports, food, travel, cars, advertising, agony page and TV listings.

This activity can be linked to English and Art and Design.

Useful Websites
See page 139.

MATHEMATICS

Activity One
Copy the grid below from the board. Write the numbers in the squares along the top row of the grid and down the left-hand side.

Now fill in the blank squares by adding the two corresponding numbers together.

	2	3	4	5
2				
3				
4				
5				

The number of squares and the numbers for the pupils to work with will depend on the age and ability of the group. They should not need calculators for this activity. The younger and less able the pupils, the fewer the squares. The numbers provided can be any size and do not need to be consecutive. You could vary the activity by asking pupils to subtract, multiply or divide the numbers provided.

Activity Two
The final score in a football match was 3–2. What could the score have been at half-time?

The aim of this activity is for pupils to identify as many different half-time scores as they can think of, e.g. 0–0, 0–1, 1–0, 1–1 etc.

Activity Three
You have been given one of each English coin. What amounts can be made using these coins?

Activity Four
Use the digits 1, 2, 3, 4, 5, 6, 7, 8 and 9 to solve the magic square. All the rows, columns and diagonals must add up to 15.

	9	
3		
		6

Answer:

4	9	2
3	5	7
8	1	6

A magic square is one where all the numbers add up to the same total on all the rows, columns and diagonals. Younger pupils may need number lines to help them.

Activity Five
Make a 2D shape picture.

If you have shapes available in your classroom, you can ask the pupils to draw a picture, on which they then label the different shapes and count how many of each shape they have used.

Activity Six
How many sums can you make using the numbers on the board? You can use + - x or ÷.

Write a selection of numbers on the board and an answer, e.g. 5, 15, 2, 100, 7, 3, 20, 10. Answer = 10. Pupils should then write as many combinations as they can find using the numbers, e.g. 7 + 3, 20 x 5 ÷ 10 etc. The numbers provided can be adapted to suit the age and ability of the pupils.

Activity Seven
Choose a number. How many sums can you do to make that number your answer?

This is similar to Activity Six, but the pupils can use any numbers to reach their answer.

Useful Websites
See page 139.

SCIENCE

Activity One
Who can tell me how many people in the class have brown eyes? How can we find out what other colour eyes there are in the class?

Ask pupils to conduct a survey of eye colour (or hair colour) in their class. They should record the results in a tally chart, and then construct a pictogram or bar chart to show the results (mathematics). If computers are available the results could be recorded and charts produced using suitable programmes (ICT).

Activity Two
We are surrounded by all sorts of different materials that have been used to make different things. Before we can decide which material is best for making something, we have to find out what its properties are, and if these are suitable for the object we are making.

The properties we are going to look at today are hardness, strength and flexibility. The materials we are going to look at are plastic, paper, rubber and steel.

Examples of these materials should be in the classroom in the form of rulers, A4 paper, rubber bands and paper clips.

Hardness can be tested through cutting or scratching, strength by attempting to break the object, and flexibility by bending.

Activity Three
We are going to test a material for its hardness, strength and flexibility.

You all have two pieces of paper. I want you to take one piece of paper and roll it into a tight tube. Put a small piece of tape on it to stop it unravelling.

Now I would like you to compare the two pieces of paper for the properties of hardness, strength and flexibility.

Prepare this activity by giving every pupil two pieces of identical paper and a small amount of tape. This activity can be used as an example of how changing a material can change its properties, and testing properties at the same time. Conclude by explaining that some shapes are stronger than others, e.g. squares and sheets are weaker than tubes and triangles.

This could be extended into a Design and Technology activity by making a tower using the paper tubes joined together in triangles.

Activity Four
Draw a picture of the human body. Label the main body parts.

The shape of the body could be drawn by asking a pupil to lie on a piece of sugar paper and drawing around them. This activity can be extended by asking the pupils to describe what each part of the body does.

Activity Five
Draw a picture of your face. Write labels for the different parts of your face.

This activity can be introduced on its own or as an extension to Activity Four. Once pupils have completed their pictures they can be asked to describe what each part of the face does. An alternative activity is to ask them to compare their face with the face of an animal, and to explain why there are differences, e.g. why does a bird have a beak and feathers instead of a mouth and skin?

Useful Websites
See page 139.

Secondary School Activities

ART AND DESIGN

Each of the activities has been written so that it can be given as it is to the class.

Alternatively, you may wish to adapt it to suit the age and ability level of the class, or to suit your own preferences and level of expertise.

Possible adaptations are suggested in italics.

Activity One
I will read out the description of an item that I would like you to sketch. You will need to listen carefully and draw as I speak. I will repeat the description to give you time to visualise the item.

Once the pupils have finished their drawing they can be asked to reveal the results.

This activity can be used with all age groups, and time and time again with the same class, as long as the item being described is different.

This activity could be extended by asking pupils to think about how they would describe everyday objects to be drawn by others.

Activity Two
Draw a picture of yourself.

You may wish to make this more specific, for example asking pupils to draw themselves:
(a) from head to foot
(b) head only
(c) using imagery to represent their personality and/or interests.

An alternative would be for pupils to draw their neighbour.

Activity Three
Draw a sketch of the person described.

This activity requires you to provide a description of someone famous, e.g. a pop or film star, or a well-known fictional character.

Activity Four
Make simple line drawings of parts of the classroom, e.g. door frames, window frames, floor covering, bricks, stonework.

Activity Five
Draw a floor plan of the school, or part of the school. Write notes on your thoughts about the design, for example in terms of space, materials, flow of movement, sound, surfaces.

This could be a floor plan of the school as it is, or how pupils would like it to be. When thinking about issues like space and flow of movement, they should be encouraged to think about how the school is used and the changing needs at different times of the day.

Activity Six
Draw a picture representing the weather.

You could specify the type of weather, for example a sunny day, a wet and/or windy day, or you could add a twist, for example a storm in a teacup.

Activity Seven
Draw a landscape.

This could be based on a view from a window, a verbal description provided by you, or, if books are available in the classroom, pupils could research their own ideas.

This activity could be extended by asking pupils to draw a landscape at two different times of the year.

Activity Eight
Select one of the items listed by your teacher.

Draw this object in at least two different styles, e.g. representational and abstract.

The items selected could include a table, chair, paintbrush, shoe, bag, can of drink.

Activity Nine
Select three items and explore ways of arranging the objects into interesting compositions.

Think about what you can do to alter the composition.

An example of three items might be a piece of paper, a pen and a pencil sharpener. Pupils could make their composition different by ripping up the paper, scrunching it up into a ball or folding it.

They could also look at the effect of light on the composition (e.g. direction and strength of light and the resulting shadows).

Activity Ten
Work in pairs. Make a series of quick sketches of each other in dramatic poses.

Try to capture quickly the essence of the pose and expression.

In order to emphasise the need for these to be quickly executed, you may wish to set a time limit.

This activity could be adapted by asking pupils to concentrate on unusual angles, close-ups, or to concentrate on expression or gesture only.

Activity Eleven
Select a person or event that could be celebrated through a mural or statue.
- Explain why you have chosen that person or event.
- Identify who the statue or mural would be for, i.e. the audience.
- Describe the style that you think would be most appropriate for that audience.
- Specify the size, scale, proportions and materials.
- Draw sketches to explain your ideas and concepts.

Activity Twelve
This is the start of a painting or drawing.

Complete the image, using your own imagination, in either a representational or abstract style. Use lettering, shapes and colours.

You can draw any combination of lines on the board or on pieces of paper given to individual pupils.

Useful Websites
See page 139.

BUSINESS STUDIES

Each of the activities has been written so that it can be given as it is to the class.

Alternatively, you may wish to adapt it to suit the age and ability level of the class, or to suit your own preferences and level of expertise.

Possible adaptations are suggested in italics.

Activity One
Choose an advertisement that you have seen in a newspaper, heard on the radio or seen on television.

Describe:
- the product
- the target audience
- what the advertisers are selling (e.g. image, sex appeal, security, etc).

This activity could be extended by asking pupils to design their own advertisement for the product concerned.

Activity Two
Compare the styles of adverts used in different publications. Think about why different styles are used, and why different products are advertised in different publications.

This activity is best if you have access to a variety of different types of newspapers and/or magazines.

Activity Three
Select a product that you can buy from a supermarket.
- Develop a new advertising campaign for that product.
- Design an advertisement for a newspaper or magazine.
- Write a script for a 10-second TV advertisement.
- Describe possible public relations (PR) events to promote the product (e.g. a famous person visiting a supermarket).
- Design point-of-sale (POS) material for the product (e.g. buy one get one free, or 50% extra).

You might wish to select just one of the options from the list above for the class to concentrate on, as each could take a whole lesson.

Activity Four
Two friends have come to you for help. They want to set up a small garden centre together but do not know where to start. What advice can you give them?
- Business ownership: partnership or limited company?
- Source of finance: do they have enough money, or do they need to think about loans and grants or selling shares?
- Personnel: how many staff? How will the business be structured?
- Marketing: how are they going to promote their business?
- Product: what are they going to sell?
- Location: where are they going to set up their business and why?

This activity could be tackled by splitting the class into groups, with each group focusing on a different aspect of the business.

The activity could be adapted by changing the type of business, e.g. bakery, garage, café etc.

Lower-ability groups could focus on the marketing aspect of this activity, by designing leaflets and posters etc.

Activity Five
You and some friends are planning to open a fashion shop. Your target audience is teenagers. You want to find out about the buying habits of your target market.

Design a questionnaire that will help you to decide on the style of your outlet (e.g. decor and music) and the type of stock you should be selling (e.g. brand names, prices, styles).

This question could be adapted to any type of business, e.g. pet shop, cleaning business, take-away.

Activity Six
Two friends who have recently set up a new music shop need advice on how to promote their business. They cannot even agree on a name. Please advise them.
- Draft a marketing strategy for your friends.
- Suggest two or three names for the business.
- Design a business card.
- Produce a brochure or leaflet.
- Write a 5 to 10-second advert for the local radio station.

This activity could be adapted to any type of business, e.g. stationery shop, flower shop, restaurant. Several of the above ideas could last a whole lesson.

Activity Seven
"The love of money is the root of all evil." 1.Timothy 6:10.

Discuss this quote from the Bible from a business perspective. Can it also be a good thing?

Activity Eight
"Attitude determines altitude." Anon.

Discuss this in terms of business success. How could this apply to successful business people such as Richard Branson (Virgin) and Bill Gates (Microsoft)?

Activity Nine
You have been given the task of selling one of the following: an odd shoe, an old newspaper, a piece of chewing gum.

Prepare a five-minute presentation to promote your product to the rest of the class.

This works well if the pupils can be encouraged to think about the possible unique selling proposition/point (USP) of their product, e.g. could someone famous have owned the shoe? Does the newspaper cover a significant event? Did someone famous chew the gum?

Activity Ten
E-commerce has affected the profit of many high-street businesses. Discuss the advantages and dis-advantages of buying online for the individual, businesses and the economy.

This could be introduced as a debate or set as an essay. The class could be divided into three groups, one looking at the issue from the perspective of the individual, one looking at businesses, and the third group looking at this in terms of the economy.

Useful Websites
See page 139.

DANCE

Each of the activities has been written so that it can be given as it is to the class.

Alternatively, you may wish to adapt it to suit the age and ability level of the class, or to suit your own preferences and level of expertise.

Possible adaptations are suggested in italics.

Activity One
Design a health-and-safety poster suitable for a dance studio.

The poster should include reference to suitable footwear, comfortable clothing, clear and safe work/floor space, warming-up and cooling-down exercises, spatial awareness, and respect for others.

Activity Two
Design a word search, including the following words:

tribal	ballet	jazz	ballroom	contemporary
disco	salsa	tap	flamenco	folk

You may wish to add further suggestions of your own, or ask pupils to add ideas of their own.

Activity Three
Work in pairs.

Choose a tune that you and your partner know and like.

Design a dance routine for two or three people that reflects the mood and tempo of the tune.

Activity Four
You have been asked to talk to Year 6 pupils about Dance.

Think about what you would tell them, for example what they will learn, what skills they need, and how to do well in the subject.

Activity Five
You have been asked to put together a dance to perform in front of Year 6 pupils.

The aim of the performance is to show the pupils what they will learn in Dance, what skills they will need, and how they can do well in the subject.

Activity Six
Think about two different dance styles.

Design a two-minute dance routine in each of these styles on the theme of happiness.

You can identify your own theme or ask the pupils to choose one of their own. Possible dance styles could be contemporary, tribal or folk. Pupils could be asked to perform their routines for the other pupils. They could then be asked to comment on each other's performances.

Useful Websites
See page 139.

DESIGN AND TECHNOLOGY (D&T): FOOD

Each of the activities has been written so that it can be given as it is to the class.

Alternatively, you may wish to adapt it to suit the age and ability level of the class, or to suit your own preferences and level of expertise.

Possible adaptations are suggested in italics.

Activity One
Make a list of foods, one for each letter of the alphabet. Include a brief description of what each one is and/or draw a picture of each.

Possibilities include apple, beetroot, cucumber, doughnut, egg, fish, grape, haddock, ice cream, jelly, kebab, lemon, milk, nut, orange, pineapple, quiche, rice, strawberry, tomato, Ugli fruit, vinegar, waffle, xanthan gum (a thickener in ice cream and dairy products), yoghurt, zabaglione.

Activity Two
Make a list of cooking equipment and serving equipment relating to a specified meal.

Draw pictures of each item and write a brief explanation of how each is used.

Activity Three
Design a questionnaire to identify people's likes or dislikes relating to a specific type of food, e.g. salad, soup, sandwiches, hot snacks, yoghurt, cake.

You might want to guide pupils to include questions about packaging, price, taste, texture, smell, competition, appearance etc. If there is time, pupils could ask each other their questions and analyse the results.

Activity Four
Design a dish. Describe it in terms of the five senses. Draw and label the individual ingredients and the meal as it would be presented.

Activity Five
- Design a new dish. This could be a healthy salad, snack or soup.
- List any ingredients you think you might use.
- Draw and label the individual ingredients.
- Describe how each ingredient would be prepared, e.g. chopped, grated, puréed.

Ideas for snack dishes could be sandwiches, yoghurt or cake.

Activity Six
Design a vegetarian menu for a take-away, restaurant or café.

Activity Seven
Design a word search or crossword relating to types of food (e.g. dairy, meat, spices, vegetables), equipment found in a kitchen, or types of places to eat.

Activity Eight
Design a menu. Describe the type of food outlet it would be suitable for and the target audience, and think about prices.

Activity Nine
You have produced a new-flavour crisp. Design the packaging. What information do you think you should include on the packet?

Activity Ten
Produce preliminary design ideas for a new ready-prepared meal.

Include a list of possible ingredients. Design the packaging.

Activity Eleven
Think about ready-prepared meals that can be bought from supermarkets and other shops.

Draw a table with columns for products, main ingredients, producer, packaging, and storage.

List any products you know about and complete as many details as you can.

Activity Twelve
Think about well-known food products that have been adapted to extend the product range.

Make a table, listing the product and the 'new' product(s).

A good example to give pupils is that of chocolate bars that have been redesigned into bigger bars, mini-bars, ice-cream bars and drinks.

Activity Thirteen
Select a well-known food product and make suggestions as to how it could be adapted to extend the original product range.

Select one option and develop it further. Describe the original and new product.

This activity can be extended by asking pupils to design the packaging for the 'new' product, to describe the features that will show it is linked to the original product and to explain how they will make it clear that it is also different.

Activity Fourteen
You have been asked to design a selection of meals suitable for serving to air passengers.

You have been invited to a meeting to discuss the brief.

Make a list of questions that you will need to ask to find out the details of the brief you will be working to.

An alternative would be to make the meals suitable for school dinners, for a restaurant, or for a motorway service station. Issues to clarify should include price, storage, preparation times, serving requirements etc.

Activity Fifteen
Design a selection of meals suitable for serving to air passengers.

Describe each aspect of the meals, including reasons for your choices. Take into account the need to cater for customers with special dietary requirements.

Activity Sixteen
Design a health-and-safety notice suitable for a food-preparation area.

Useful Websites
See page 139.

DESIGN AND TECHNOLOGY (D&T): RESISTANT MATERIALS

Each of the activities has been written so that it can be given as it is to the class.

Alternatively, you may wish to adapt it to suit the age and ability level of the class, or to suit your own preferences and level of expertise.

Possible adaptations are suggested in italics.

Activity One
Write a list of joining techniques, the materials for which they are suitable and how they are used.

Pupils could be asked to produce this as a chart suitable for display in a D&T room.

Activity Two
Write a list of D&T equipment and a brief description of how each item is used.

Draw a picture of each item.

Activity Three
Design a container to hold something fragile or precious.

Make a list of containers. Identify what they contain, what they are made from, their size (approximate) and shape. List anything you think is good or bad about each one.

Draw a number of possible designs for your containers.

Write a list of tools and equipment that might be used to make your container. Draw and label each one.

Design a marketing campaign to promote your product.

It is useful to start with a discussion about containers in general and containers for fragile and precious things, including nature's best example, an egg. Other examples might be a jewellery box, a safe, a cat basket.

Although they will not be making their design, pupils should be encouraged to work on designs that are realistic.

Any one of the above could fill a lesson, depending on age and ability.

Activity Four
Design a product, taking into account the appearance, function, safety and reliability of the item.

Draw preliminary sketches, list materials, tools and equipment, and suggest possible processes.

If the class is working on QCA Unit 8A, the pupils may be working on a new computer mouse, a foldable structure to hold tools, or a kite that incorporates a logo and a mechanism for storing and releasing the string.

Once you have found out what the pupils have been working on, you can decide whether to focus on that or point them towards something completely different, such as a CD/DVD holder.

Activity Five
Design a folding chair. Produce preliminary sketches.

Identify the target age group, and where, when and how the chair will be used.

List the materials from which it will be made, the tools and equipment required and the processes involved in manufacture.

Examples could include chairs for the beach, a small office, or a children's playgroup.

Activity Six
Make a list of characteristics and working properties of the materials on the board.

Describe a list of items in terms of the materials used in their manufacture, and their properties.

The materials listed could include: aluminium, card, mdf, mild steel, pewter, plastic and plywood.

Activity Seven
Construct three free-standing structures from newspaper, which will support a lightweight exercise book.

Test the structures to find out which is the strongest. (You may need to test to destruction.)

Write a description of how each structure was made, and a comparison.

Explain how each was tested, which was the strongest and why you think this was the case.

Activity Eight
Produce a poster for the D&T room on health and safety.

Include Dos and Don'ts for safe handling of specific tools and equipment.

Activity Nine
Design a word search relating to D&T. Test it on your friends when it is completed.

You could ask pupils to focus on specific aspects of D&T, e.g. materials, joining techniques, or processes.

Activity Ten
Choose an item in the room.

Redesign it for a specific market.

Think about practical, aesthetic and safety issues.

Rather than letting pupils choose an item and a market, you might prefer to specify an item and market so they are all working on the same thing.

Activity Eleven
Design a carton for a take-away meal.

It must be:
- made from a single A4 sheet of paper or card
- easy to assemble
- easy to fold flat
- able to hold the food without leaks or spills.

Try two or three designs.

Draw a net of your chosen design and assemble.

Useful Websites
See page 139.

DESIGN AND TECHNOLOGY (D&T): TEXTILES

Each of the activities has been written so that it can be given as it is to the class.

Alternatively, you may wish to adapt it to suit the age and ability level of the class, or to suit your own preferences and level of expertise.

Possible adaptations are suggested in italics.

Activity One
Design an item of clothing or an accessory.

Produce a number of sketches showing possible designs.

You may find it helpful to specify a type of clothing or accessory, or a potential market for the designs. Ideas include designing fashion wear suitable for a teenage market, an item of clothing suitable for a baby up to the age of two, or a hat suitable for Royal Ascot.

Activity Two
Develop a questionnaire to find out about current fashions, popular brand names, styles, colours, trends and prices, relating to a specific garment or accessory.

Pupils who complete the design of their questionnaire can be asked to collect responses from their classmates and to analyse the results.

Activity Three
Write a list of existing products that are examples of a specific garment or accessory.

Sketch examples of the different styles currently available.

You may need to focus pupils' attention on a particular type of clothing or accessory. Examples could include wedding dresses, sportswear or belts.

Activity Four
Choose an item of clothing or accessory that you have designed or made.

Design a marketing campaign to promote your chosen item of clothing or accessory.

Pupils could focus on a campaign in a magazine, or they could be encouraged to think about other media such as television, radio and poster advertising.

Activity Five
Identify possible tools and equipment needed to produce the garment or accessory of your choice.

List, draw and label each item on your list.

An alternative for this activity would be for pupils to design a poster identifying the tools and equipment needed.

Activity Six
Think of a specific type of garment or accessory.

Make a list of the types of these garments or accessories that are already available.

Identify the purpose and describe the main features of these garments or accessories.

Activity Seven
Make labelled sketches of three or four ideas for a specific type of garment or accessory.

Identify its benefits to the target market.

List details of any other similar products on the market.

Describe the reasons why your designs are better.

Activity Eight
Design a slogan or image that can be reproduced on a T-shirt, hat or scarf.

Explain how this would need to be adapted to be reproduced on a key ring, pen or drink mat.

Provide labelled sketches to support your explanation.

Activity Nine
Design a new uniform for the school.

Annotate your designs, explaining practical considerations versus creative and aesthetic considerations.

Alternatives include a new uniform for a local or national sports team, or outfits for a new band or dance group.

Activity Ten
Design a purse, wallet or pencil case.

List the types of materials and fastenings you could use.

Describe the materials and fastenings you wish to use in your design and give reasons for your choices.

Pupils should be encouraged to think about and list the advantages and disadvantages of the various types of material and fastenings.

Activity Eleven
Design headwear for a wedding.

Specify the sex and age of the wearer and the style of the occasion on which the hat will be worn.

Develop detailed designs. Label your sketches to identify colours, fabrics and decorative features.

Explain the inspiration behind your ideas.

Alternatives could be to design headwear for an Easter parade, fancy dress party, carnival or Royal Ascot.

Activity Twelve
Produce a number of sketches focusing on a single feature of one of your designs, e.g. a fastening or a section of the pattern.

This activity could be introduced as an extension to any of the above activities, or as a stand-alone activity.

Useful Websites
See page 139.

DRAMA

Each of the activities has been written so that it can be given as it is to the class.

Alternatively, you may wish to adapt it to suit the age and ability level of the class, or to suit your own preferences and level of expertise.

Possible adaptations are suggested in italics.

Activity One
Choose a soap opera.

Write a script for the next episode.

This is a good activity for pupils to work on in groups. Once they have written their scripts they can have time to rehearse and then, if appropriate, act out a scene in front of the rest of the class. It is worth emphasising that there should be no body contact – especially where pupils are writing fight scenes.

Activity Two
Act out an episode of your favourite soap opera or a scene from your favourite film.

See comments above.

Activity Three
Someone has stolen something from you.

Write a short script dealing with this situation.

Now write a second script showing a different way of dealing with the same situation. Act out the two scenarios.

Activity Four
"I hate you!"

Think about who might have said this and why. How did they say it? What led up to these words? What happens next?

This could be the stimulus for an improvisation, a mime or a dramatic performance. It could also lead to pupils writing a short play, or it could be linked into a film, television or radio performance.

Activity Five
Draw a cartoon strip outlining a scene for an animated film or cartoon for television.

This could be based on an episode at school or a cartoon or animated film that the pupils have recently seen.

Activity Six
Choose a current event. Dramatise it.

Pupils could choose to write about a current event as a scene for a soap opera, a musical, an animated film, a horror story, a romance etc.

You might prefer to choose the event yourself so that pupils can get on with the activity rather than wasting time trying to agree which event to focus on.

Useful Websites
See page 139.

ENGLISH

Each of the activities has been written so that it can be given as it is to the class.

Alternatively, you may wish to adapt it to suit the age and ability level of the class, or to suit your own preferences and level of expertise.

Possible adaptations are suggested in italics.

Activity One
Look at the newspaper articles you have been given.

Think about the language used in each.

Rewrite one of the articles in a different style for another paper.

This activity is based on articles from old newspapers, which you can tear up and give out to individuals or groups. The idea is to rewrite an article found in a tabloid in a style more suited to a serious newspaper, and vice versa.

Activity Two
Write a letter introducing yourself to me.

Tell me about your personality, your likes and your dislikes.

This is a good activity to do with a class that you have not met before.

Pupils who finish quickly can add a description of their physical appearance.

Activity Three
Look at the newspaper article you have been given.

Identify nouns, verbs, adjectives, prepositions etc.

This activity uses articles from old newspapers, which you can tear up and give out to individuals or groups. Pupils who finish quite quickly can be given other articles to look at.

Activity Four
Read the newspaper article you have been given.

Write your own article about a particular event.

This activity uses articles from old newspapers, which you can tear up and give out to individuals or groups.

Activity Five
Look at the newspaper article you have been given.

Separate fact from supposition in the article.

This activity is based on articles from old newspapers, which you can tear up and give out to individuals or groups. Tabloid newspapers are particularly good for this exercise.

Activity Six
Write a descriptive piece about the school.

This is going to be read by parents and children thinking about coming to this school.

An alternative activity is to ask pupils to write two descriptive pieces, one suitable for prospective pupils and one for their parents.

Activity Seven
Write directions to help me find my way around the school.

I need to be able to find reception, the staff room and the library.

This activity is best for younger age groups.

The class can be divided into small groups, with each group given a different destination. When they have finished writing, the directions can be read out so the others can guess where they are going.

With older groups, alternative destinations can be given that are further afield, or the activity can be introduced as a descriptive piece: 'My Journey to ....'

Activity Eight
Write an article for the school magazine, e.g. 'New Teacher Arrives in School'.

Pupils could be asked to write one realistic article and one fictional article.

Activity Nine
Write a short story.

Pupils could be allowed to choose their own subject or you could suggest one, e.g. mysterious teacher arrives in school; I arrived at school and no one else was there; or based on their holidays.

Activity Ten
Write a poem about yourself.

Other possible themes include the school, the sea, the seasons, a holiday, a famous person or an historic event.

Activity Eleven
Write a speech about something you feel strongly about.

Encourage pupils to think about why they are making a speech and who the audience is. It might be something related to school, e.g. should they wear uniforms? or it could be related to something in the news.

Encourage them to use repetition to help emphasise a point, and to include emotive language, using words they think will help prompt an emotional response in those listening.

Activity Twelve
Write a short play on 'My First Day at School'.

You might wish to guide pupils as to the style, e.g. romantic, thriller, dramatic, suspense, science fiction.

You could give alternative ideas for the title, e.g. 'My Last Day at School', 'The Most Important Day in My Life'.

Useful Websites
See page 139.

FRENCH

Each of the activities has been written so that it can be given as it is to the class.

Alternatively, you may wish to adapt it to suit the age and ability level of the class, or to suit your own preferences and level of expertise.

Possible adaptations are suggested in italics.

Introduction
It is always useful if you can greet the class – even if that is the limit of your French.

Some useful phrases:

Hello	*Bonjour*
Hello, how are you?	*Bonjour, ça va?*
My name is ….	*Je m'appelle ….*
Can I go to the toilet?	*Est-ce que je peux aller à la toilette?*
Be quiet!	*Taisez-vous!*
Yes	*Oui*
No	*Non*

Activity One
List one word for as many letters of the alphabet as you can. Write each word in French and English.

Pupils might need to use French–English dictionaries to be able to do this.

Activity Two
Design a calendar. Draw a picture for each month. Label the picture in French.

Pupils could be encouraged to draw pictures to do with religious festivals, or weather-related pictures, which they then label.

Activity Three
Draw a picture of yourself. Label the picture in French.

Activity Four
Design a word search with 10 French words hidden among the letters. Swap this with your neighbour when you have finished.

Pupils can use words found in displays on the walls, in French dictionaries if available, or in their textbooks. If they are stuck, write some words on the board (e.g. one to ten).

Activity Five
Working in teams of four, find the following words. Write down the English and French for each.

Write any words you like on the board. These can be on a specific theme or a random selection. This activity relies on textbooks, dictionaries and/or online computers being available.

Activity Six

Use the glossary in your textbooks to help you write a quiz for the rest of the class. You must know the answers to any questions you set. For example:

- a room beginning with c (e.g. *cuisine* = kitchen)
- the English for e.g. *homme* (man)
- a building beginning with g (e.g. *gare* = railway station)
- a family member beginning with p (e.g. *père* = father)
- the days of the week (*lundi, mardi, mercredi, jeudi, vendredi, samedi, dimanche*).

You can add to or adapt the suggested list as appropriate to the group. This activity works best if dictionaries, textbooks and/or online computers are available.

Activity Seven

Find these adjectives in the glossary of your textbook or dictionary. Draw a table to show which are positive and which are negative.

Write any adjectives you like on the board, e.g. angry, boring, clever, dirty, easy, hard, kind, lazy, mean, nice, quiet, soft, tired. This activity relies on textbooks, dictionaries and/or online computers being available.

Activity Eight

List the names of as many countries as you can think of. Look in your French textbook and dictionary to find out the names in French and write them down. Find out as many capital cities as you can and write them down in English and French.

This activity works best if textbooks and dictionaries are available. If computers are available, you could also ask pupils to research and draw the countries' flags.

Activity Nine

Design a crossword with the clues in English and the answers in French.

A more difficult alternative would be for the clues to be in French and the answers in English.

Activity Ten

Divide your page into four. Write down the words for the four seasons in the boxes. Draw a picture in each box representing the weather for that season. Label the picture in French. Use your French dictionary to find the words if you need to.

Activity Eleven

Divide your page into two columns. Make a list of as many types of transport as you can think of. Use the glossary in your textbook and a French dictionary to find the French translation of each, and complete your table.

Pupils who complete this activity quickly could be asked to draw pictures of each mode of transport.

Activity Twelve

Divide your page into three columns. Make a list of all the types of clothes you can think of. Use the glossary in your textbook and a French dictionary to find the French translation for each. Complete your table. Draw a picture of each type of clothing.

Activity Thirteen

In which other countries is French spoken? What do you know about these countries? What would you like to know? Produce a brochure providing information about one of the countries.

This activity works best if computers are available.

Useful Websites

See page 139.

GEOGRAPHY

Each of the activities has been written so that it can be given as it is to the class.

Alternatively, you may wish to adapt it to suit the age and ability level of the class, or to suit your own preferences and level of expertise.

Possible adaptations are suggested in italics.

Activity One
Draw a plan of the school to help newcomers and visitors. Remember to include doors.

Think about health and safety, for example include the fire escapes.

Pupils who complete this activity quickly could be asked to write directions to specific areas, for example the library, canteen, sports hall.

Activity Two
Write a description of your local area.

Write it in the form of an advertisement, brochure or poster encouraging people to visit or to move to your area.

Include natural and human features, for example any information you can think of about transport, amenities, housing and parkland.

Activity Three
Design a quiz about England, Wales, Scotland and Northern Ireland. These will be tested on the rest of the class. You must know the answer to any questions that you include in your quiz.

You could provide the following questions as possible starting points:
1. Name the capital cities of England, Wales, Scotland and Northern Ireland.
2. Name the longest river in the UK.
3. Name the longest river in England, Wales, Scotland and Northern Ireland.
4. How long is the coastline of mainland Great Britain?
5. Name the patron saint of England, Wales, Scotland and Northern Ireland.

The answers are: 1. London, Cardiff, Edinburgh, Belfast; 2. Severn; 3. Thames, Towy, Tay, Bann; 4. 11072.76 miles or 17819.88 km (as measured along Mean High Water); 5. St George, St David, St Andrew, St Patrick.

You may prefer to ask the pupils to concentrate on the local area.

Activity Four
Describe the weather on a typical day in each of the different seasons.

Younger pupils could be asked to draw a picture to support each description.

Pupils who finish this activity could be asked to describe the benefits and drawbacks of each type of weather. This could be natural benefits, e.g. rain helping crops to grow, or economic benefits, e.g. rain creates sales of umbrellas, raincoats etc.

Activity Five
Make a list of as many shops as you can think of in your local area.

Make a table showing the type of shop and what is sold in that shop.

An extension to this activity could be to ask pupils to think about what type of shop they would set up and why. How would it benefit the local area?

Activity Six
Explain what is meant by 'crime'.

Make a list of as many types of crime as you can think of. Discuss your list with your partner.

Can you think of categories for these crimes?

Explanations of crime should include the idea of an act against people or property punishable by law. You may need to suggest categories, such as crimes against people or crimes against property.

Activity Seven
Write a brief explanation of 'tourism'.

Classify different types of holiday, e.g. at home, abroad, sightseeing, touring, beach, ski-ing, full-board, self-catering, camping.

Activity Eight
Tourism can be seasonal, i.e. people will only want to visit a place at a particular time of year.

What sort of holidays do you think will be seasonal?

Make a list of jobs that are most likely to be affected by the seasonal demands of tourism.

Access to computers will help this activity.

Activity Nine
Select a country.

Find out as much information as you can relating to the human and physical features of that country.

Produce a leaflet, poster or brochure promoting that country to a specific target audience.

You may find it useful to specify a particular target audience, e.g. skiers, campers, pilgrims, people with a specific interest.

Access to computers will help this activity.

An alternative would be to relate this to a city, county or specific area within a country.

Activity Ten
Design a questionnaire to find out about people's holiday choices.

Ask questions that will help you to find out where people have been on holiday, what they enjoy about holidays, where they would most like to go on holiday in the future, and what affects their choices about holidays.

Conduct your survey and record your results.

Factors affecting choices may include weather, costs, people and family.

Useful Websites
See page 139.

GERMAN

Each of the activities has been written so that it can be given as it is to the class.

Alternatively, you may wish to adapt it to suit the age and ability level of the class, or to suit your own preferences and level of expertise.

Possible adaptations are suggested in italics.

Introduction

It is always useful if you can greet the class – even if that is the limit of your German.

Some useful phrases:

Hello	*Hallo*
Hello, how are you?	*Wie gehts?*
My name is …	*Ich heisse …*
Can I go to the toilet?	*Darf ich zu die Toiletten gehen?*
Be quiet!	*Konnen Sie ruhig sein!*
Yes	*Ja*
No	*Nein*

Activity One

List one word for as many letters of the alphabet as you can. Write each word in German and English.

Pupils might need to use German–English dictionaries to be able to do this.

Activity Two

Design a calendar. Draw a picture for each month. Label the picture in German.

Pupils could be encouraged to draw pictures to do with religious festivals, or weather-related pictures, which they then label.

Activity Three

Draw a picture of yourself. Label the picture in German.

Activity Four

Design a word search with ten German words hidden among the letters. Swap this with your neighbour when you have finished.

Pupils can use words found in displays on the walls, in German dictionaries if available, or in their textbooks. If they are stuck, write some words on the board (e.g. one to ten).

Activity Five

Working in teams of four, find the following words. Write down the English and German for each.

Write any words you like on the board. These can be on a specific theme or a random selection. This activity relies on textbooks, dictionaries and/or online computers being available.

Activity Six
Use the glossary in your textbooks to help you write a quiz for the rest of the class. You must know the answers to any questions you set. For example:

- a room beginning with k (e.g. *Küche* = kitchen)
- the English for e.g. *Junge* (boy)
- a building beginning with b (e.g. *Bahnhof* = railway station)
- a family member beginning with v (e.g. *Vater* = father)
- the days of the week (*Montag, Dienstag, Mittwoch, Donnerstag, Freitag, Samstag, Sonntag*).

You can add or adapt the suggested list as appropriate to the group. This activity works best if dictionaries, textbooks and/or online computers are available.

Activity Seven
Find these adjectives in the glossary of your textbook or dictionary. Draw a table to show which are positive and which are negative.

Write any adjectives you like on the board, e.g. angry, boring, clever, dirty, easy, hard, kind, lazy, mean, nice, quiet, soft, tired. This activity relies on textbooks, dictionaries and/or online computers being available.

Activity Eight
List the names of as many countries as you can think of. Look in your German textbook and dictionary to find out the names in German and write them down. Find out as many capital cities as you can and write them down in English and German.

This activity works best if textbooks and dictionaries are available. If computers are available, you could also ask pupils to research and draw the countries' flags.

Activity Nine
Design a crossword with the clues in English and the answers in German.

A more difficult alternative would be for the clues to be in German and the answers in English.

Activity Ten
Divide your page into four. Write down the words for the four seasons in the boxes. Draw a picture in each box representing the weather for that season. Label the picture in German. Use your German dictionary to find the words if you need to.

Activity Eleven
Divide your page into two columns. Make a list of as many types of transport as you can think of. Use the glossary in your textbook and a German dictionary to find the German translation of each, and complete your table.

Pupils who complete this activity quickly could be asked to draw pictures of each mode of transport.

Activity Twelve
Divide your page into three columns. Make a list of all the types of clothes you can think of. Use the glossary in your textbook and a German dictionary to find the German translation for each. Complete your table. Draw a picture of each type of clothing.

Activity Thirteen
In which other countries is German spoken? What do you know about these countries? What would you like to know? Produce a brochure providing information about one of the countries.

This activity works best if computers are available.

Useful Websites
See page 139.

HISTORY

Each of the activities has been written so that it can be given as it is to the class.

Alternatively, you may wish to adapt it to suit the age and ability level of the class, or to suit your own preferences and level of expertise.

Possible adaptations are suggested in italics.

Activity One
Work in groups. Write five quiz questions – you MUST know the answers. These questions will be posed to the rest of the class.

This can be extended into a much longer activity simply by requiring pupils to write more questions and then posing the questions to the rest of the class.

Activity Two
Draw a timeline of your own life (this could be developed by asking pupils to project into the future). Significant dates could be illustrated in an appropriate way, e.g. picture of baby to illustrate the birth of a sibling.

An alternative to this is to draw a timeline of their day. It can be very detailed: have breakfast, clean teeth, brush hair etc.

Activity Three
Design a word search. Hide the following words: chronological, century, era, empire, period, past, source, interpretation, site, relevance, timeline, historical.

Activity Four
Design a crossword about significant historical events.

Activity Five
Design a word search including the following words: medieval, Middle Ages, Black Death, Peasants' Revolt, manor, Domesday Book, tithes, villain, reeve, demesne, Christendom, monastery, pilgrimage, relic, priest, heretic, purgatory.

Activity Six
The *Domesday Book* gives us detailed information about England in 1086. What would you write about in a modern edition of the *Domesday Book*?

Activity Seven
What do we mean by 'the vote'? At what age should people be entitled to vote? Should this apply to everyone of that age?

Activity Eight
Choose an historical event that you think is particularly significant. Produce a poster explaining what happened, and why you believe it to be significant.

You might prefer to identify a small number of events for pupils to choose from.

Activity Nine
Choose one person who you think has made an important contribution to life in Britain. Produce a mini-biography of that person, providing information about them, their life and their achievements.

Useful Websites
See page 139.

Information and Communication Technology (ICT)

Each of the activities has been written so that it can be given as it is to the class.

Alternatively, you may wish to adapt it to suit the age and ability level of the class, or to suit your own preferences and level of expertise.

Possible adaptations are suggested in italics.

Activity One
Write notes about where we use computers in everyday life.

You might find that you need to give pupils hints, e.g. shops, manufacturing industries, offices.

Pupils can be asked to support their work with illustrations from Clip Art (found in Insert – Picture – Clip Art), or with information found by searching online.

Activity Two
Write a list of what we use computers for, e.g. writing, calculations, drawing, computer control.

Compare this with how these functions would have been undertaken in the past.

Pupils can be asked to support their work with illustrations from Clip Art (found in Insert – Picture – Clip Art), or with information found by searching online.

Activity Three
Log on to www.teach-ict.com.

This website has a number of quizzes suitable for pupils of all ages that entertain, test and reinforce pupils' ICT knowledge. They can be used as an introductory activity, or a combination of the activities can be used to fill a whole lesson.

I have found Dunkin' Teacher and Hangman good for all ages. Twister is better for older and more able groups, Catch the Fruit and Balloon Attack are better for younger and less able groups.

Activity Four
Log on to www.reviseict.co.uk.

This website gives access to useful quizzes and revision sections that can be used to test and reinforce pupils' ICT knowledge.

Each game relates to a specific unit, so once you have established the age of the class it should be fairly straightforward to find appropriate activities.

Activity Five
Log on to www.bbc.co.uk/schools/gcsebitesize/ict.

This website is particularly relevant for GCSE classes.

It provides revision notes and tests on ICT systems, hardware, software, data communications, databases, measurement and control, modelling, the legal framework and implications of ICT, and even has a mock exam that can be printed off for pupils to try.

Activity Six
Log on to www.ictgcse.com.

This website is useful for GCSE classes.

Activity Seven
Use Word to produce a brochure on:

- ICT in the school
- ICT and how it is used in everyday life.

Activity Eight
Do a Google search for the following terms.

Type in the definitions and suggested alternative terms, and find supporting images.

computer	disk	personal computer	ROM
database	disk drive	CPU	hard drive
spreadsheets	broadband	RAM	input device
mouse	floppy disk	storage device	printer

Pupils should know to type in 'define:' before any word for which they want a definition. There should not be a space between the colon and the word to be defined. You can give them extra words if you wish to broaden the search.

Activity Nine
Use Publisher to produce a flier on:

- your local area: include details of local attractions
- yourself: why pupils should vote for you to represent the class.

Activity Ten
Use PowerPoint to produce a multimedia presentation on:

- the school: to be presented to parents of Year 6 pupils
- ICT in school: to be presented to Year 6 pupils.

Activity Eleven
Produce a PowerPoint presentation on:

- the history of the computer
- the history of the internet
- options for Years 8 and 9.

Pupils can use search engines such as Google to search for information. Useful sites (at the time of writing) are:

- *for the first presentation: www.computerhistory.org and www.pbs.org/nerds/timeline*
- *for the second presentation: www.walthowe.com/navnet/history.html and www.wbglinks.net/pages/history.*

Activity Twelve
Use Word or Publisher to produce a greetings card, e.g. for a birthday, anniversary, leaving card, congratulations.

If you are happier using Word, interest can be added to a Word document by using special effects. These can be found by going to Format – Font – Text Effects. Pupils could also experiment by adding a theme (Format – Theme).

Activity Thirteen
This is the first time I have met you. I would like to know something about you. So I would like you to produce a PowerPoint presentation about yourself. You could include slides on such things as your likes and dislikes, your hobbies, your family, your pets and your friends.

This activity could be done as a letter and CV using Word or a leaflet using Publisher.

Useful Websites
See page 139.

MATHEMATICS

Each of the activities has been written so that it can be given as it is to the class.

Alternatively, you may wish to adapt it to suit the age and ability level of the class, or to suit your own preferences and level of expertise.

Possible adaptations are suggested in italics.

Activity One
Copy the letters of the alphabet and the corresponding numbers below.

A	B	C	D	E	F	G	H	I	J	K	L	M	N	O	P	Q	R	S	T	U	V	W	X	Y	Z
1	2	3	4	5	6	7	8	9	10	11	12	13	14	15	16	17	18	19	20	21	22	23	24	25	26

Use this information to calculate the numerical value of your first name.

For example, Anne will be 1+14+14+5 = 34.

As an extension, having calculated their first name, pupils can then be asked to calculate their last name, their address, and/or the name of their favourite pop/soap opera/film star.

They can also be asked to calculate the numerical value of their name if they subtract their first name from their last name, or vice versa.

For older and more able groups, multiplication and division can be used instead of addition.

Pupils working in pairs can be asked to calculate a value for their name using addition, subtraction, division and multiplication. They can then tell their partner the end value. Their partner then has to work out how the total was arrived at.

Activity Two
Copy the grid below from the board. Write the numbers in the squares along the top row of the grid and down the left-hand side.

Now fill in the blank squares by multiplying the two corresponding numbers together.

	2	3	4	5
2				
3				
4				
5				

The number of squares and the numbers for the pupils to multiply will depend on the age and ability of the group. They should not need calculators for this activity. The younger and less able the pupils, the fewer the squares.

	6	9	3	2
7				
9				
1				
3				

You can use any numbers.

Variations on this theme would be for the pupils to add, subtract, or even divide the numbers provided.

Activity Three
Draw as many shapes as you can with an area of 12 cm^2.

This activity is best done on squared paper.

A variation of this activity is for pupils to draw as many shapes as they can think of with a perimeter of 12 cm.

Activity Four

Copy the grid below. For each row, multiply the first two numbers and add the third.

1	2	3
4	5	6
7	8	9

Draw a grid on the board with nine boxes as shown in the example above. Put a number in each box from 1 to 9. These can be in any order. Pupils must multiply the first and second number and add the third. In the example above, this would be 1 x 2 + 3 = 5.

For younger and less able groups, put the number 1 in the middle and low numbers in the middle columns.

Pupils can be asked to work from right to left, and left to right, up and down, and diagonally in all directions.

Activity Five

Use a calculator to find three consecutive numbers that, when multiplied together, would give you answers to the following questions. Write down the three numbers and the answer.

e.g. a number between 100 and 150 = 4 x 5 x 6 = 120
or a number that is divisible by 8 = e.g. 4 x 5 x 6 = 120 ÷ 8 = 15; or 6 x 7 x 8 = 336 ÷ 8 = 42

- a number between 700 and 800
- the nearest possible number to 500
- the smallest possible number over 1500
- an odd number
- a number without an 0 in it
- a number with 2 digits that are the same
- a number that is divisible by 6
- Can every number that is divisible by 6 be the product of three consecutive numbers?

Activity Six

The final score in a football match was 3–2. What could the score have been at half-time?

The aim of this activity is for pupils to identify as many different half-time scores as they can think of, e.g. 0–0, 0–1, 1–0, 1–1.

Activity Seven

You have been given one of each English coin. What amounts cannot be made using the available coins?

Activity Eight

Pentominoes are shapes made from five squares joined together, full side to full side, e.g. Can you find all 12?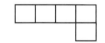

This activity can be extended to look at hexominoes, which are shapes made using six squares.   There are 35.

Activity Nine

Solve the following magic square using the numbers 1, 3, 6, 7 and 9 to add up to 26.

1	3	6	7	9
3	7	9	6	1
9	6	3	1	7
6	1	7	9	3
7	9	1	3	6

Magic squares are grids in which the numbers in each row, column and diagonal add up to the same total. Draw this grid on the board. The amount of numbers you provide will depend on the age and ability of the pupils.

This activity can be simplified by using smaller grids (see page 101) and providing more numbers, or made more difficult by using larger grids and providing fewer numbers.

Pupils could be asked to design their own square and test it out on other pupils in the class.

Useful Websites

See page 139.

MEDIA

Each of the activities has been written so that it can be given as it is to the class.

Alternatively, you may wish to adapt it to suit the age and ability level of the class, or to suit your own preferences and level of expertise.

Possible adaptations are suggested in italics.

Activity One
Select a film of your choice.

Describe it in terms of: the main story line, main characters, audience, fiction or non-fiction, special effects, stars, genre.

This activity could be developed by asking pupils to write an analysis of why they believe the film was successful.

Activity Two
Select an advertisement to analyse.

What is the product being advertised?

What image is the product given in the advert?

Who is it aimed at?

Is it an advert for TV, radio, press?

Redesign your own version of the advert for a different media and/or audience.

Activity Three
Select a magazine.

Describe the target readership for this magazine.

Identify the competition.

List the advertisers, naming the product and the manufacturers.

If you were responsible for increasing the advertising in the magazine, what sort of companies/products do you think you would approach, and why?

Pupils could be asked to imagine that they have been appointed the new editor for the magazine. What changes would they make and why?

Activity Four
Plan the front page of a newspaper.

Think about the position, size and style of the headline, the columns and pictures.

The starting point is the design and layout of the paper, but you might want to provide the pupils with front page news to include in the newspaper, or begin with a discussion of current news.

The activity could be developed so that pupils produce two front pages, one for a tabloid and a second for a serious newspaper.

Activity Five

Identify a tabloid newspaper.

Choose a current event to write an article about.

Write the article in a style suitable for this newspaper.

Now write about the same event but in a style more suited to a serious newspaper.

Activity Six

Write a two-minute script for a soap opera of your choice.

Remember to set the scene, describe the characters, write the dialogue and give stage directions.

Activity Seven

Select a popular, long-running soap opera.

Write an analysis of the soap opera, explaining why you think it has remained popular for so many years.

Pupils may need to be prompted to mention such things as characters, storylines, issues, quality of writing and use of humour.

Useful Websites

See page 139.

MUSIC

Each of the activities has been written so that it can be given as it is to the class.

Alternatively, you may wish to adapt it to suit the age and ability level of the class, or to suit your own preferences and level of expertise.

Possible adaptations are suggested in italics.

Activity One
Choose a popular tune.

Write your own lyrics to be sung to this tune.

Include at least two verses and a chorus.

Activity Two
Work in pairs to write ten questions for a music quiz.

You must know the answers to each question, as these will be posed to the rest of the class.

Possible adaptations include specifying a particular area of music for the pupils to focus on, dividing the class into teams with each group focusing on different areas for their questions, or setting your own questions.

A few sample questions that could be used are listed below.

1. *What is an orchestra?*
2. *List the four main sections of an orchestra.*
3. *Name two instruments you would find in the string section.*
4. *Name an instrument you would find in the woodwind section.*
5. *What instruments do you find in the brass section?*
6. *What instruments do you find in the percussion section?*
7. *What is the name of the person who leads the orchestra?*
8. *What was Mozart's full name?*
9. *What do the terms soprano, alto and tenor relate to?*
10. *Complete these styles of music by filling in the missing letters: j – – z, r – g – a –, – o – s e.*
11. *What is the name of this symbol? (Draw a picture of a treble clef).*
12. *What is the longest running television programme about popular music?*
13. *What is an opera?*
14. *How many people are in a quintet?*
15. *Name an instrument that might make you think about an ice cream.*

Possible answers: a large group of people playing instruments; strings, woodwind, brass, percussion; violin, viola, cello or double bass; flute, piccolo, clarinet, oboe, saxophone or bassoon; French horn, trumpet, tuba, trombone; cymbals, snare drum, timpani, bass drum; the conductor; Wolfgang Amadeus Mozart; voice pitch; jazz, reggae, house; treble clef; 'Top of the Pops'; a dramatic performance set, sung and performed to music; five; cornet.

Activity Three
Produce a word search using the following words:

acoustic	electronic	sampler	synthesised	delay
reverb	vocoder	analogue	digital	multi-track
recording	minidisc	tape	microphone	stereo

This activity is particularly suitable for Year 7. If computers or appropriate books are available, pupils could also be asked to find the meaning of each word.

Activity Four
Produce a word search using the following words:

pitch	higher	lower	phrase	rondo
shorter	texture	timbre	longer	pulse
duration	tempo	rhythm	metre	verse
chorus	round	ostinato	pentatonic	repetition

This activity is particularly suitable for Year 7. If computers or appropriate books are available, pupils could also be asked to find the meaning of each word.

Activity Five
Produce a word search using the following words:

chord	mode	major	minor	tempo
metre	inversion	retrograde	ornamentation	overture
ostinato	mnemonics	rhythm	blues	motif
riff	diatonic harmony	hook	verse	chorus
ballad	sequence	lyrics	melody	fanfare

This activity is particularly suitable for Year 8. If computers or appropriate books are available, pupils could also be asked to find the meaning of each word.

Activity Six
Produce a word search using the following words:

asthayi	refrain	antara	stanza	rag
tal	mukhra	discord	resolution	major
minor	chromaticism	dynamics	timbre	texture
concerto	grosso	tutti	virtuoso	cadenza
concertante				

This activity is particularly suitable for Year 9. If computers or appropriate books are available, pupils could also be asked to find the meaning of each word.

Activity Seven
Discuss how and when music is used to create an intended effect, for example in films and advertisements.

Discuss the use of various aspects of the music, such as the structure and lyrics, and the importance of each.

What do you think is gained by using music in these situations?

In this activity pupils should be encouraged to think about the use of music in films and advertisements they have seen at the cinema or on television.

Activity Eight
Where is music used?

Where do you hear it?

Why is it there?

What is it trying to achieve? How does it make you feel?

In this activity pupils could be encouraged to think about the use of music in shops and on telephones.

Useful Websites
See page 139.

PERSONAL SOCIAL AND HEALTH EDUCATION (PSHE)

Each of the activities has been written so that it can be given as it is to the class.

Alternatively, you may wish to adapt it to suit the age and ability level of the class, or to suit your own preferences and level of expertise.

Possible adaptations are suggested in italics.

Activity One

As this is the first time I have met you, I would like to find out more about each of you. To help me to do this, I would like you all to produce a description of yourself and the person sitting next to you. You can use words or pictures to describe yourself. Do not show your partner your descriptions until you have finished. Now compare your descriptions about each other. What does this tell you about how you see yourself, the characteristics you feel are important and how other people see you?

This activity may need to be monitored carefully.

Activity Two

Write a letter describing your life to someone the same age as you living in another country, for example:

- a person in Africa or India
- a person in Greenland or Alaska
- a person in America.

Now write a response from their perspective, describing what you think their life will be like.

This could be done as though the letters are between pen friends.

Activity Three

Write a diary entry or poem from the perspective of people living in the same country, but of different ages, for example:

- yourself
- someone in their 30s
- someone in their 70s.

Activity Four

Try to look at a situation from someone else's point of view:

- Incy Wincy Spider climbing up the spout
- the wolf in *Red Riding Hood*
- one of the ugly sisters in *Cinderella*.

Write a diary as if it were written by each of these characters.

Activity Five

Design a snakes and ladders game for your life.

Start at birth and go up to any age.

Think about the achievements or landmarks that you have achieved or would like to achieve, e.g. learning to walk, first day at school, passing your driving test, first job. Mark these with the 'ladders' that take you forward in your game. Then think about possible disappointments that have happened or might happen, e.g. failing an exam or falling out with a friend, and mark these with the 'snakes' that take you backwards in your game.

Useful Websites

See page 139.

PHYSICAL EDUCATION (PE)

Each of the activities has been written so that it can be given as it is to the class.

Alternatively, you may wish to adapt it to suit the age and ability level of the class, or to suit your own preferences and level of expertise.

Possible adaptations are suggested in italics.

Activity One
Design a word search using the following words:

hockey	cricket	lacrosse	tennis	badminton
football	rugby	netball	rounders	basketball
team	players	side	referee	score

Activity Two
Write a description of a sport of your choice for someone who knows nothing about it. Include details of the number of people involved, the aim of the game and the rules.

Activity Three
Write a job description for a referee for a sport of your choice. What are the benefits of the job? What qualities are required?

Activity Four
Design a word search using the following words:

starts	set plays	competitions	fitness	officiating
restarts	team play	preparation	activity	attack
team	tournaments	recovery	leading	defence
opponent	exercise	referee	whistle	strategy

Activity Five
Devise a training regime (include details about diet and exercise) for a specific sporting event.

Activity Six
Design a programme for the school's sports day.

Activity Seven
JK Rowling made up the game 'Quidditch' in the *Harry Potter* books. Make up a game of your own. Write the rules. Describe the equipment. How many people are involved? What is the aim of the game?

Activity Eight
Design a poster or leaflet promoting a healthy diet.

Activity Nine
Nominations are being invited for Sportsperson of the Year. Put forward your nomination and give reasons.

Pupils could be asked to nominate someone in their class, school or in the public arena.

Useful Websites
See page 139.

RELIGIOUS EDUCATION (RE) / RELIGIOUS STUDIES (RS)

Each of the activities has been written so that it can be given as it is to the class.

Alternatively, you may wish to adapt it to suit the age and ability level of the class, or to suit your own preferences and level of expertise.

Possible adaptations are suggested in italics.

Activity One
List all the words you can think of associated with justice.

Describe examples of justice, e.g. in a school context, at home, in religious terms, in the world.

Think about examples of injustice (e.g. people wrongly imprisoned).

Describe how you would feel if you were the victim of injustice.

You may need to provide pupils with examples of words associated with justice, including fairness, crime, and punishment.

Activity Two
Choose a religious figure. Research their life.

Describe the person and the major events in their life. Summarise why you think this person is important.

This activity can be based on pupils' current knowledge of a religious figure. Further research could be undertaken if textbooks, religious texts and/or computers are available.

Activity Three
Make a list of religious festivals. Select one.

Design a poster or leaflet explaining its religious significance, and how and why the festival is still celebrated today.

This activity is best done if textbooks, religious texts and/or computers are available.

Activity Four
How and why do different religions celebrate the birth of a baby?

Produce a poster or leaflet explaining the key parts of the different celebrations.

Pupils could be encouraged to focus on one religion or to compare two or more religions. This may depend on the availability of textbooks, religious texts and/or computers.

An alternative would be to ask pupils to compare the celebration of marriage or other significant events, such as welcoming people into the faith.

Activity Five
Each religion has a set of guiding principles by which its followers try to live.

Choose a religion and describe its principles.

If appropriate, pupils could also be asked to write their own list of rules to live by.

Useful Websites
See page 139.

SCIENCE

Each of the activities has been written so that it can be given as it is to the class.

Alternatively, you may wish to adapt it to suit the age and ability level of the class, or to suit your own preferences and level of expertise.

Possible adaptations are suggested in italics.

Activity One
Use one sheet of A4 paper to make a bridge. Test it.

Provide a written explanation of what you have done and what happens when you test the bridge.

You may prefer to specify the span of the bridge. You may also wish to provide additional materials for pupils to use when building the bridge, e.g. paper clips.

Activity Two
Design a word search of scientific terms.

You may prefer pupils to focus on one area of science, e.g. chemistry, biology, or to be even more specific, e.g. looking at the subject area they have just studied in science. Examples of more specific word searches are provided below.

This activity can be made more challenging by asking pupils to write clues that have to be solved to find out which words are hidden in the word search. Once they have designed the word search, this can be exchanged with another pupil to solve the clues and find the words.

Activity Three
Obesity can be a serious threat to the health of many people in the western world.

Design a poster about obesity and health.

An alternative would be for pupils to produce a leaflet.

Activity Four
Identify the five senses.

Explain why it is important for us to have these senses.

What happens if we lose one or more of these senses?

Choose an animal and describe how its senses are important to its survival.

An extension of this activity could be to draw pictures to illustrate and explain how the senses work.

Activity Five
Design a word search with the following words: lungs, heart, diaphragm, rib cage, breathing, respiration, air, inhale, exhale.

An extension of this activity could be to ask pupils to write an explanation of how these words are connected.

Activity Six
Design a word search using the following words: diet, nutrients, vitamins, calcium, iron, protein, energy, disease, obesity, anorexia, rickets, scurvy.

An extension of this activity could be to ask pupils to write an explanation of how these words are connected.

Activity Seven
What do you understand by the term 'fit'? How could you find out whether a person is fit? Discuss how fitness means different things to different people, e.g. a sportsperson unable to play because they are not fit.

Activity Eight
Design a fitness programme.

Describe the part each of the following play in that programme: exercise, diet, smoking, alcohol, sleep.

Activity Nine
Write a script for a radio talk-show about a current scientific issue.

You may wish to suggest a number of possible subjects.

Activity Ten
Write a poem called 'My Favourite Experiment'.

An extension for this activity would be for pupils to write an essay on their favourite experiment.

Activity Eleven
Choose ten favourite possessions.

Describe them, including what they are made from, and explain why you think these materials were used.

This activity could be extended by asking pupils to discuss other materials that could be used to make the items and their properties.

Activity Twelve
Design a poster with an 'anti-smoking' message.

Alternatives could be to ask pupils to produce a leaflet on this subject, or suggest other subjects such as: drink-driving, drugs, recycling, healthy eating/balanced diet.

Activity Thirteen
Think of a scientific word for every letter of the alphabet.

Explain its meaning and give an example of its use in a sentence.

Activity Fourteen
Write ten challenging questions about a scientific topic. Leave three lines between each question.

When pupils have finished writing their questions they could swap with another pupil to answer their questions. Then they could swap back to mark the answers (or swap with a different pupil).

Activity Fifteen
Construct a mind map of a topic you have studied in science.

Pupils could be asked to do this for the last topic they have studied.

Activity Sixteen
Invent a new environment. Describe it. Design an animal or plant to live there. Explain the ways in which it has adapted to its environment.

You could introduce this activity by discussing how polar bears have adapted to the cold climate in which they live.

Useful Websites
See page 139.

SPANISH

Each of the activities has been written so that it can be given as it is to the class.

Alternatively, you may wish to adapt it to suit the age and ability level of the class, or to suit your own preferences and level of expertise.

Possible adaptations are suggested in italics.

Introduction
It is always useful if you can greet the class – even if that is the limit of your Spanish.

Some useful phrases:

Hello	*Hola*
Hello, how are you?	*Hola, cómo es usted?*
My name is ….	*Mi nombre es …*
Can I go to the toilet?	*Puedo ir al tocador?*
Be quiet!	*Sea reservado!*
Yes	Si
No	No

Activity One
List one word for as many letters of the alphabet as you can. Write each word in Spanish and English.

Pupils may need to use Spanish–English dictionaries to be able to do this.

Activity Two
Design a calendar. Draw a picture for each month. Label the picture in Spanish.

Pupils could be encouraged to draw pictures to do with religious festivals, or weather-related pictures, which they then label.

Activity Three
Draw a picture of yourself. Label the picture in Spanish.

Activity Four
Design a word search with ten Spanish words hidden among the letters. Swap this with your neighbour when you have finished.

Pupils can use words found in displays on the walls, in Spanish dictionaries if available, or in their textbooks. If they are stuck, write some words on the board (e.g. one to ten).

Activity Five
Working in teams of four, find the following words. Write down the English and Spanish for each.

Write any words you like on the board. These can be on a specific theme or a random selection. This activity relies on textbooks, dictionaries or online computers being available.

Activity Six
Use the glossary in your textbooks to help you write a quiz for the rest of the class. You must know the answers to any questions you set. For example:

- a room beginning with c (e.g. *cocina* = kitchen)
- the English for e.g. *hombre* (man)
- a building beginning with f (e.g. *ferrocarril* = railway station)
- a family member beginning with p (e.g. *padre* = father)
- the days of the week (*lunes, martes, miércoles, jueves, viernes, sábado, domingo*).

You can add or adapt the suggested list as appropriate to the group. This activity works best if dictionaries, textbooks and/or online computers are available.

Activity Seven
Find these adjectives in the glossary of your textbook or dictionary. Draw a table to show which are positive and which are negative.

Write any adjectives you like on the board, e.g. angry, boring, clever, dirty, easy, hard, kind, lazy, mean, nice, quiet, soft, tired. This activity relies on textbooks, dictionaries and/or online computers being available.

Activity Eight
List the names of as many countries as you can think of. Look in your Spanish textbook and dictionary to find out the names in Spanish and write them down. Find out as many capital cities as you can and write them down in English and Spanish.

This activity works best if textbook and dictionaries are available. If computers are available, you could also ask the pupils to research and draw the countries' flags.

Activity Nine
Design a crossword with the clues in English and the answers in Spanish.

A more difficult alternative would be for the clues to be in Spanish and the answers in English.

Activity Ten
Divide your page into four. Write down the words for the four seasons in the boxes. Draw a picture in each box representing the weather for that season. Label the picture in Spanish. Use your Spanish dictionary to find the words if you need to.

Activity Eleven
Divide your page into two columns. Make a list of as many types of transport as you can think of. Use the glossary in your textbook and a Spanish dictionary to find the Spanish translation of each, and complete your table.

Pupils who complete this activity quickly could be asked to draw pictures of each mode of transport.

Activity Twelve
Divide your page into three columns. Make a list of all the types of clothes you can think of. Use the glossary in your textbook and a Spanish dictionary to find the Spanish translation for each. Complete your table. Draw a picture of each type of clothing.

Activity Thirteen
In which other countries is Spanish spoken? What do you know about these countries? What would you like to know? Produce a brochure providing information about one of the countries.

This activity works best if computers are available.

Useful Websites
See page 139.

WEBSITES

This section is provided in case you are lucky enough to be forewarned about the subjects you are going to be covering, or have a cover lesson in a classroom with computers.

Primary School

www.bbc.co.uk – provides online learning, support, advice and links to other useful sites

www.channel4.com/learning – provides programme notes and interactive websites covering history, mathematics, music, PSHE, RE and science for ages 5–11

www.firstschoolyears.com – provides free worksheets, flashcards and other resources for Key Stage 1 and lower Key Stage 2

www.ngfl.gov.uk – provides access to a wide range of resources for primary school education

www.literacymatters.co.uk – provides ideas and resources for teaching literacy from Reception to Year 7

www.schoolzone.co.uk – provides evaluations and reviews of thousands of resources

www.songsforteaching.com – provides lyrics, sound clips and teaching suggestions

www.teachingideas.co.uk – provides ideas, activities and worksheets for the primary school age group

www.teachit.co.uk – provides ideas for teaching English

www.teachernet.gov.uk/teachingandlearning/ – provides teaching ideas, resources and reviews of lesson plans

www.tes.co.uk – provides a selection of lesson plans and worksheets

Secondary School

Art and Design
www.bbc.co.uk/learning – provides information and links to other useful sites on art and design, history of art, definitions of art terms and more

www.schoolzone.co.uk – provides evaluations and reviews of resources

www.teachernet.gov.uk/teachingandlearning/ – provides teaching ideas, resources and reviews of lesson plans

Business Studies
www.bbc.co.uk/learning – provides information and links to other useful sites, including *GCSE Bitesize Business Studies*, up-to-date business news and business advice

www.schoolzone.co.uk – provides evaluations and reviews of resources

Dance
www.bbc.co.uk/learning - *Performing Arts* – provides information and links to other useful sites, including *Blast-Dance*

www.schoolzone.co.uk – provides evaluations and reviews of resources

Design and Technology (D&T)
www.channel4.com/learning – provides programme notes and interactive websites concerned with the design and development of a number of products

www.schoolzone.co.uk – provides evaluations and reviews of resources

Drama
www.bbc.co.uk/learning - *Performing Arts* – provides information and links to other useful sites, including *Stagework,* which gives behind-the-scenes experience of the theatre

www.schoolzone.co.uk – provides evaluations and reviews of resources

English

www.bbc.co.uk/learning – provides information and links to other useful sites, including *GCSE Bitesize English,* a guide to genres and context, a grammar guide and free online texts

www.channel4.com/learning – provides programme notes and interactive websites about authors and their books, writing, punctuation and more

www.schoolzone.co.uk – provides evaluations and reviews of resources

www.teachernet.gov.uk/teachingandlearning/ – provides teaching ideas, resources and reviews of lesson plans

www.teachit.co.uk – provides ideas for teaching English

French

www.babelfish.altavista.com/tr – provides an online translation service

www.bbc.co.uk/learning - *Languages* – provides information and links to other useful sites, including online courses, news, features, holiday information and reviews of French films

www.channel4.com/learning - *Languages* – provides programme summaries and transcripts, grammar exercises and activities

www.channel4.com/learning - *Languages - Extra* – provides interactive activities

www.schoolzone.co.uk – provides evaluations and reviews of resources

www.songsforteaching.com – provides lyrics, sound clips and teaching suggestions

www.teachernet.gov.uk/teachingandlearning/ – provides teaching ideas, resources and reviews of lesson plans

Geography

www.channel4.com/learning – provides programme notes on environmental issues and more

www.schoolzone.co.uk – provides evaluations and reviews of resources

www.teachernet.gov.uk/teachingandlearning/ – provides teaching ideas, resources and reviews of lesson plans

German

www.babelfish.altavista.com/tr – provides an online translation service

www.bbc.co.uk/learning - *Languages* – provides information and links to other useful sites

www.channel4.com/learning - *Languages - Extra* – provides interactive activities

www.schoolzone.co.uk – provides evaluations and reviews of resources

www.songsforteaching.com – provides lyrics, sound clips and teaching suggestions

www.teachernet.gov.uk/teachingandlearning/ – provides teaching ideas, resources and reviews of lesson plans

History

www.bbc.co.uk/learning - *History* – provides information and links to other useful sites, including history trails with quizzes and games, historic speeches and an archive for the Second World War

www.channel4.com/learning - *Learning* – provides programme notes and interactive websites on the Spanish Armada and the First World War

www.schoolzone.co.uk – provides evaluations and reviews of resources

www.teachernet.gov.uk/teachingandlearning/ – provides teaching ideas, resources and reviews of lesson plans

Information and Communication Technology (ICT)

www.bbc.co.uk/learning - *Information Technology* – provides information about the internet, software and digital media, key skills and links to other useful sites, including *GCSE Bitesize ICT*

www.schoolzone.co.uk – provides evaluations and reviews of resources

www.teachernet.gov.uk/teachingandlearning/ – provides teaching ideas, resources and reviews of lesson plans

Mathematics

www.bbc.co.uk/learning – provides information and links to other useful sites, including *GCSE Bitesize Maths*

www.channel4.com/learning - *Learning* – provides programme notes and interactive websites, including an interactive adventure game dealing with number, algebra, shape, space and measures

www.schoolzone.co.uk – provides evaluations and reviews of resources www.songsforteaching.com – provides lyrics, sound clips and teaching suggestions

www.teachernet.gov.uk/teachingandlearning/ – provides teaching ideas, resources and reviews of lesson plans

Media

www.bbc.co.uk/learning - *Media Studies* – provides information and links to other useful sites, and looks at broadcasting and journalism

www.schoolzone.co.uk – provides evaluations and reviews of resources

Music

www.bbc.co.uk/learning – provides information and links to other useful sites, including *GCSE Bitesize Music;* also provides information on how to succeed in the music Industry

www.schoolzone.co.uk – provides evaluations and reviews of resources

www.songsforteaching.com – provides lyrics, sound clips, and teaching suggestions

www.teachernet.gov.uk/teachingandlearning/ – provides teaching ideas, resources and reviews of lesson plans

Personal Social and Health Education (PSHE)

www.bbc.co.uk/learning - *Personal Development* – provides a look at issues relating to health and confidence

www.channel4.com/learning - *Learning PSHE* – provides programme notes and interactive websites relating to citizenship, careers, environmental issues and more

www.schoolzone.co.uk – provides evaluations and reviews of resources

www.teachernet.gov.uk/teachingandlearning/ – provides teaching ideas, resources and reviews of lesson plans relating to citizenship

Physical Education (PE)

www.bbc.co.uk/learning – provides information and links to other useful sites

www.channel4.com/learning - *Learning* – provides programme notes and interactive websites

www.schoolzone.co.uk – provides evaluations and reviews of resources

www.teachernet.gov.uk/teachingandlearning/ – provides teaching ideas, resources and reviews of lesson plans

Religious Education (RE) / Religious Studies (RS)

www.bbc.co.uk/learning - *Religious Studies* – provides information on different religions and ethics, and links to other useful sites, including *GCSE Bitesize Religious Studies*

www.schoolzone.co.uk – provides evaluations and reviews of resources

www.teachernet.gov.uk/teachingandlearning/ – provides teaching ideas, resources and reviews of lesson plans

Science

www.bbc.co.uk/learning – provides information and links to other useful sites relating to all aspects of science

www.channel4.com/learning - *Learning* – provides programme notes and interactive websites

www.schoolzone.co.uk – provides evaluations and reviews of resources

www.songsforteaching.com – provides lyrics, sound clips and teaching suggestions

www.teachernet.gov.uk/teachingandlearning/ – provides teaching ideas, resources and reviews of lesson plans

Spanish

www.babelfish.altavista.com/tr – provides an online translation service

www.bbc.co.uk/learning – provides information and links to other useful sites

www.channel4.com/learning - *Languages - Extra* – provides interactive activities, and can access programme summaries and transcripts, grammar exercises and activities

www.schoolzone.co.uk – provides evaluations and reviews of resources

www.songsforteaching.com – provides lyrics, sound clips and teaching suggestions

www.teachernet.gov.uk/teachingandlearning/ – provides teaching ideas, resources and reviews of lesson plans

Supply Agencies

The following is a selection of supply agencies in the United Kingdom. It is not intended to be an exhaustive list. See also, the advertisements at the front of The Supply Teacher and The School Cover Co-ordinator sections.

Name of Agency	Website Address
A4E Education	www.a4eeducation.co.uk
Ambition 24 Hours Education	www.supply-agency.co.uk
Capita Education Resourcing	www.capitaers.co.uk
Career Teachers	www.careerteachers.co.uk
Celsian Education	www.celsiangroup.com
Chalkface Recruitment Ltd	www.chalkfaceltd.co.uk
Class Supply	www.class-supply.co.uk
Connex Education	www.connex-education.com
Cover Teachers	www.coverteachers.co.uk
Day to Day Teachers	www.daytodayteachers.com
Dream Education	www.dream-group.com
Education Recruitment Network	www.ernteachers.co.uk
Education Staffing Solutions	www.educationstaffingsolutions.co.uk
eteach	www.eteach.com
First for Education	www.firstforeducation.co.uk
G B Recruitment	www.gbrs.co.uk
Head Line	www.headline-uk.com
ITN Teachers	www.itnteachers.com
Just Teachers	www.justteachers.co.uk
Keep Education	www.keepeducation.co.uk
Kelly Educational Staffing	www.kellyservices.co.uk
Key Stage Supply	www.keystagesupply.co.uk
Long Term Teachers	www.longtermteachers.com
Louis Paul Recruitment	www.louis-paul.com
Mark Education	www.markeducation.co.uk
Masterlock	www.masterlock.co.uk
Oasis (Staffwise)	www.oasis-recruitment.co.uk
Premiere People	www.premierepeople.com
Protocol Teachers	www.protocol-teachers.com
Quality Locums Education	www.qualitylocums.com
Quay Education Services	www.quayeducation.co.uk
Reed Education Professionals	www.reed.co.uk/education
Renaissance Education	www.edulon.co.uk
Select Education plc	www.selecteducation.com
Standby Teacher Services	www.standbyteachers.com
STC Consortium	www.stcconsortium.co.uk
Step Teachers	www.stepteachers.co.uk
Supply Desk	www.supplydesk.co.uk
Supply Teachers.com	www.supplyteachers.com
TAP	www.tap.ltd.com
Teach London	www.teachlondon.com
Teach Web	www.teachweb.co.uk
Teaching Agency	www.teaching-agency.co.uk
Teaching Personnel	www.teachingpersonnel.com
The Education Network	www.t-e-n.co.uk
Timeplan	www.timeplan.com
TPP Newman	www.tpp.co.uk
Tradewind Recruitment	www.twrecruitment.com
Trust Education	www.trusteducation.co.uk
UK Teaching	www.uk-teaching.co.uk

Recruitment and Employment Confederation (REC)

Education Sector Group – Code of Practice

The Recruitment and Employment Confederation Education Sector Group members specialise in the placement of supply teachers throughout the UK.

All members are required to comply with the REC Education Sector Group Code of Practice, which is reproduced below.

The Code of Practice is binding on all members of the Education Sector Group of the Recruitment and Employment Confederation. Complaints against members of the REC Education Sector Group will be investigated by the REC Professional Standards Manager under both this Code of Practice and the general REC Code of Good Recruitment Practice.

The Education Sector Group code has been established to set out clearly the responsibilities of employment businesses providing Teachers and Support Workers to LEAs and schools in both the public and private sector.

In this code the following definitions apply:

Agency: The Employment Business, being a member of the Education Sector Group of the REC, which is providing the services of a Teacher or Support Worker to a Client.

Client: The LEA, school, college or other place of learning contracting with the Agency for the supply of the services of the Teacher/Support Worker and responsible for supervising, directing and controlling the Teacher/Support Worker.

Teacher: An individual supplied by the Agency to work under the supervision, direction or control of the Client in a teaching capacity.

Lecturer: An individual supplied by the Agency to work under the supervision, direction or control of the Client (college or other place of learning) in a lecturing capacity.

Support Worker: An individual supplied by the Agency to work under the supervision, direction and control of the Client including but not limited to classroom assistants, administrators, catering staff and janitors.

Staff: Individuals engaged by the Agency to work on the Agency's premises under the Agency's direction and control in the operation of the Agency including but not limited to the Agency's directors, managers, recruitment consultants, researchers, administrators and accountants.

General

Mandatory Obligations
Agencies will ensure that all Staff are aware of and comply with the provisions of the:

- Employment Agencies Act 1973 and its associated Conduct Regulations;

- Child protection provisions of the Criminal Justice and Court Services Act 2000;

- Education Reform Act 1988;

- Protection of Children Act 1999;

- Education (Restriction of Employment) Regulations 2000; as well as other relevant legislation and guidance including the:

- Department for Education and Skills Circular 7/96 setting out the rules relating to the provision of supply teachers;

- Department for Education and Skills letter to Teacher Employment Agencies and Businesses dated March 2002 entitled "Guidance about Criminal Record and List 99 Checks via the Criminal Records Bureau";

- Data Protection Act 1998; and

Statutory provisions relating to equal opportunities, discrimination, taxation and health and safety and any other statutory provision or Code of Practice that is applicable to the operation of an Agency supplying workers to schools and children's education establishments from time to time. Where a provision in this Code is less stringent than that of the general REC Code of Good Recruitment Practice, the relevant provision of the general REC Code will apply.

Good Practice

1. Agencies will ensure that Staff are competent and adequately and appropriately trained to carry out their duties effectively and that records of training and development are retained by the Agency and that Staff are regularly appraised and training and development needs are regularly identified and acted upon.

2. Where a dispute exists between Agencies that cannot be satisfactorily resolved, the dispute must be referred to the REC Professional Standards Team who will endeavour to resolve the matter.

3. Complaints against Agencies by Clients, Teachers and Support Workers, which cannot be satisfactorily resolved without submission to REC will be dealt with under the REC Complaints Procedure, and where relevant, the REC Disciplinary Procedure.

4. Agencies will co-operate with each other as far as is reasonably possible by sharing Disclosure information in respect of Teachers/Support Workers registering or registered with more than one Agency. Where an Agency (B) is provided with a Teacher/Support Worker's copy of the Disclosure and they have been registered previously with another Agency (A), Agency B may make a request to Agency A asking whether they were given any further information on the Disclosure. This request can only be made with the consent of the Teacher/Support Worker. Agency A should comply with this request by confirming with Agency B whether or not the police disclosed non-conviction information that was not included on the Teacher/Support Worker's copy of the Disclosure. Agency A should not divulge the actual information. Agency B must obtain a separate Disclosure if Agency A advises that the police did disclose non-conviction information to them that was not included on the Teacher/Support Worker's copy of the Disclosure.

Agencies' Duties to Schools

Mandatory Obligations
1. Agencies must carry out reference checks in accordance with the following points:

- At least 2 current professional and/or academic references must be taken;

- References must be satisfactory and current (one must be from the most recent employer if applicable);

- References should be written and the identity of the referee verified;

- If verbal references are obtained:

  - a contemporaneous record of the name and status of the referee must be taken;

  - the identity of the referee must be independently verified;

  - the date and name of the Staff member taking the reference must be recorded;

  - the reference must be substantiated by a request for a written reference within 24 hours and a record of the request retained;

- the Client must be informed if a Teacher is being supplied before the written reference has been received back by the Agency;

- if an open written reference is received it will not be accepted until the authenticity of the reference and the identity of the referee have been verified. A contemporaneous record of the status of the referee together with the date and name of the Staff member taking the reference must be recorded.

2. Request and verify reasons for gaps in employment history in the last 10 years.

3. Check the identity of the Teacher/Support Worker, by having sight of an original utility bill or other official document showing the name and current address of the Teacher/Support Worker plus an original document such as a photo driving licence, passport or other type of photo identification. Copies of these documents must be kept on file.

4. In the case of Teachers require sight of original certificates or officially certified copy of certificates of qualification before supplying the Teacher to a Client and retain a photocopy verified with the name of the member of Staff taking the copy and the date it was taken. In the absence of original certificates, an original letter confirming qualifications from the General Training Council or the relevant training institute will suffice.

5. Obtain an Enhanced Disclosure from the Criminal Records Bureau in respect of any Teacher supplied or Support Worker supplied who is a teaching assistant (or any other individual) and may be in sole charge of children during an assignment, who is or has been resident in the UK before they are placed. An Enhanced Disclosure may include information from local police records and DfES List 99 and will state whether the Teacher is on the Protection of Children Act List or is disqualified from working with children. Obtain a Standard Disclosure from the Criminal Records Bureau in respect of any Support Worker supplied (except those falling within the provisions of clause 5 above) who is or has been resident in the UK before they are placed.

6. In the case of overseas Teachers/Support Workers obtain a notarised copy of an equivalent check carried out in their home country. In the case of overseas trained Teachers ensure that the qualifications held by the Teacher are on the UK National Academic Recognition Information Centre (NARIC) List of qualifications as being equivalent to UK NARIC standards.

7. Carry out a detailed face-to-face interview before supplying Teachers/Support Workers to clients to ensure that Teachers/Support Workers are suitable for the bookings for which they are to be submitted.

8. Provide written terms of business to the client as soon as possible after receipt of an initial booking and in any event prior to providing a Client with any services.

9. In the event that information relating to a Teacher/Support Worker comes to light after the Agency has placed a Teacher/Support Worker with a Client an Agency must, on the day the information is received or as soon after as reasonably practicable, seek the advice of the DfES Misconduct Unit in order to deal appropriately with that information. Evidence that advice has been sought must be retained by the Agency. This provision will apply even if the Teacher/Support Worker is no longer working through the Agency.

Good Practice

10. Ensure a medical declaration is completed and signed by a Teacher

11. Ensure that any complaints brought by the client are documented and dealt with in a professional manner and are acknowledged in writing within 2 working days.

Agencies' Duties to Teachers

Mandatory Obligations
Agencies will:

- Ensure that the written agreement of the Teacher/Support Worker to the Agency's current terms of engagement is obtained before the Teacher/Support Worker is provided with any work finding services.

- State without ambiguity the pay rate due to a Teacher/Support Worker before the assignment commences.

- Transmit to Teachers and Support Workers any relevant information relating to an assignment, including information relating to health and safety matters, timetable requirements, the class(es) they will be teaching/assisting in, any special needs of the children they are likely to come into contact with, any other adults who will be in the class(es) and the line management arrangements.

Good Practice
Agencies will:

- Deduct PAYE and NI from remuneration to the Teacher/Support Worker.

- Pay Teachers and Support Workers promptly and efficiently and as specified in the Agency's terms of engagement.

Glossary

The following is a selection of acronyms and terms relating to the education systems in England, Northern Ireland, Scotland and Wales.

A Level	*See* GCE A Level.
Academic Year	The academic year consists of 195 days, running from September to July in England and Wales, and August to June/July in Scotland.
ACCAC	*See* Qualification, Curriculum and Assessment Authority for Wales.
ADHD	Attention Deficit Hyperactivity Disorder is characterised by an inability to concentrate, and hyperactivity.
AST	An Advanced Skills Teacher has been recognised through external assessment as having excellent classroom practice. They are given increased non-contact time to share their skills and experience with other teachers.
B.Ed	*See* Bachelor of Education.
Bachelor of Education	A B.Ed is a degree in education. It is one of the main routes to becoming qualified as a teacher. *See also* PGCE.
Bursar	Administrator who controls the financial management of the school.
C of E	Church of England.
CAL	Computer Assisted Learning or Computer Aided Learning.
CCEA	*See* Council for the Curriculum, Examinations and Assessment.
Classroom Assistant	A member of the school staff who supports the teacher in primary, special and secondary classrooms. Also known as teaching assistant (TA), learning support assistant (LSA) or special needs assistant. Website: www.classroom-assistant.net
Community School	A state school that is open to the local community after school hours and at weekends for educational and other activities.
Comprehensive School	A secondary school that accepts students of all abilities.
Core Subjects	The National Curriculum in England and Wales includes three core subjects: English, Mathematics and Science. *See also* Foundation Subjects.
Council for the Curriculum, Examinations and Assessment	The CCEA is a non-departmental public body reporting to the Department of Education in Northern Ireland. It sets examinations, advises on what should be taught in schools, and monitors the standard of qualifications and examinations.
CPD	Continuing Professional Development.
D&T	Design and Technology.
DE	*See* Department of Education. *See also* DEL.
Degree	Examples of degrees include the BA: Bachelor of Arts; B.Ed: Bachelor of Education; and BSc: Bachelor of Science.
DEL	*See* Department for Education and Learning.
DELLS	*See* Department for Education Lifelong Learning and Skills in Wales.
Department for Education and Learning	The DEL has responsibility for further and higher education in Northern Ireland. Website: www.delni.gov.uk
Department for Education, Lifelong Learning, and Skills in Wales	DELLS, part of the Welsh Assembly Government, includes what was previously ACCAC and NATED. Website: new.wales.gov.uk/topics/educationandskills/
Department of Education	The DE is responsible for the central administration of all aspects of education and related services in Northern Ireland, except for higher and further education. Website:www.deni.gov.uk

Department of Higher and Further Education, Training and Employment	The DHFETE was one of two government departments for education in Northern Ireland. Now replaced by the DEL. *See also* DE. Website: www.nics.gov.uk/ni-direct/dhfete/
DfEE	Department for Education and Employment – now the DfES.
DfES	Department for Education and Skills (previously DfEE). The government body with responsibility for education in primary and secondary schools in England and Wales. Website: www.dfes.gov.uk
DHFETE	*See* Department of Higher and Further Education, Training and Employment.
EBD	Emotional and Behavioural Difficulties.
ELWa	Education and Learning Wales. Website: www.elwa.ac.uk
Estyn	Estyn is the Office of Her Majesty's Inspectorate for Education and Training in Wales. It aims to raise standards and quality of education and training in Wales through inspection and advice. Website: www.estyn.gov.uk
ETLLD	*See* Scottish Executive Enterprise, Transport and Lifelong Learning Department.
Extended School	A school that provides activities and services, outside the school day, for the benefit of its pupils, their families and the community.
FE	*See* Further Education.
Feeder School	This is the name given by secondary schools to the primary school(s) from which the majority of their pupils will come.
Foundation School	This is a school managed by a governing body, responsible for employing staff and setting admission criteria. The land and buildings are usually owned by the governing body or a charitable foundation.
Foundation Stage	Reception class at primary schools.
Foundation Subjects	The National Curriculum consists of nine foundation subjects: Art and Design, Citizenship, Design and Technology, Geography, History, Information and Communication Technology, Modern Foreign Languages, Music, and Physical Education. Not to be confused with Foundation stage (*see above*).
Further Education	FE covers post-compulsory education (16 – 19+). It usually refers to vocational courses undertaken at Colleges of Further Education.
GCE A Level	General Certificate of Education Advanced Level. These are usually taken at 18 or older.
GCE AS Level	General Certificate of Education, Advanced Subsidiary Level. Can be taken as a stand-alone qualification or at the end of the first year of an A Level course.
GCSE	*See* General Certificate of Secondary Education.
General Certificate of Secondary Education	The GCSE is the qualification taken by pupils at age 16 in Year 11 in England and Wales.
General National Vocational Qualification	A GNVQ is a vocational qualification, approximately equal to A Level standard.
General Teaching Council	The GTC is the professional body for teaching. There is one for England, Northern Ireland, Scotland and Wales. Websites: www.gtce.org.uk; www.gtcni.org.uk; www.gtcs.org.uk; gtcw.org.uk
GNVQ	*See* General National Vocational Qualification.
Grammar School	A secondary school with a selective entrance system.
GTC	*See* General Teaching Council.
HE	*See* Higher Education.

HI	Hearing Impaired.
Higher Education	HE refers to post-compulsory education. It usually refers to university courses.
Highers	Examinations taken by pupils in Scotland after passing standard grade qualifications.
HMI	Her Majesty's Inspectors.
HOD	Head of Department.
HOY	Head of Year.
ICT	Information and Communication Technology.
Independent School	This is also known as a public school and a private school. *See* Private School.
Independent Schools Council	Previously the Independent Schools Joint Council. ISC provides advice about, and support for, independent schools. Website: www.isc.co.uk
Induction Year	The first year of teaching after successfully gaining a teaching qualification.
Infant	Infant classes or infant schools are for 5 to 7 year-olds. The first year of infants is often called the reception class.
INSET	In-service education and training of teachers.
ISC	*See* Independent Schools Council.
ITE	Initial Teacher Education. *See* also ITT.
ITT	Initial Teacher Training. Courses that qualify someone to become a teacher, including B.Eds, PGCEs and TDA courses. *See* B.Ed, PGCE and TDA.
JMI	Junior, Middle and Infant.
Junior	Juniors are 7 to 11 year-olds. They are either taught in junior schools, or in junior classes within primary schools.
Key Stage	There are four key stages: Key Stage 1 for 5 to 7 year-olds; Key Stage 2 for 7 to 11 year-olds; Key Stage 3 for 11 to 14 year-olds; and Key Stage 4 for 14 to 16 year-olds. Further education is sometimes referred to as Key Stage 5.
KS	*See* Key Stage.
LEA	*See* Local Education Authority.
League Table	The DfES School and College Achievement and Attainment Tables (formerly Performance Tables) give information on the achievements of pupils in local schools and how they compare with other schools in the local authority area, and in England as a whole. Website: www.dfes.gov.uk/performancetables
Local Education Authority	An LEA is part of a council in England or Wales responsible for overseeing education within that council's jurisdiction.
LRC	Learning Resource Centre. The library.
LSA	Learning Support Assistant. *See* Classroom Assistant.
LSU	Learning Support Unit. An area within a school where pupils who are disaffected, at risk of exclusion or vulnerable because of family or social issues, can go for learning or emotional support. Website: www.standards.dfes.gov.uk/sie/eic/lsu/
Main Pay Scale	Teachers working in state schools are paid according to the MPS. Where they start on the scale will depend on their qualifications, experience and level of responsibility. The spine points are M1 to M6. Teachers move up to the next spine point each September. Some supply agencies pay according to the MPS; others have their own system.
Maintained School	A state school operated within the local education authority (England and Wales). Pupils are not charged to attend.
MFL	Modern Foreign Languages, including German, French, Spanish and Italian.

Middle School	In some areas pupils leave their primary schools at 8 or 9 to study at a middle school, before going on to a secondary school aged 12 or 13.
MLD	Moderate Learning Difficulties.
MPS	*See* Main Pay Scale.
NAFW	National Assembly for Wales. Website: www.wales.gov.uk
NATED	*See* National Assembly for Wales Training and Education Department.
National Assembly for Wales Training and Education Department	NATED was the government department responsible for education in Wales. *See* Department for Education Lifelong Learning and Skills in Wales. Website: new.wales.gov.uk/topics/educationandskills
National Curriculum	The NC identifies the statutory entitlement to learning for all pupils up to the age of 16. This includes content, attainment targets and assessment (*see* SATs). Website: www.nc.uk.net and www.curriculum2000.co.uk
National Literacy Strategy	A government initiative designed to raise standards of literacy in schools. Website: www.standards.dfes.gov.uk/primary/
National Numeracy Strategy	A government initiative designed to raise standards of mathematics in schools. Website: www.standards.dfes.gov.uk/numeracy
NAW	National Assembly for Wales.
NC	*See* National Curriculum.
NFER	National Foundation for Educational Research. Website: www.nfer.ac.uk
NQT	Newly Qualified Teacher.
Nursery	Nurseries provide care for pre-school children. They are not part of the education system. Not to be confused with nursery schools. *See* below.
Nursery School	A nursery school provides non-compulsory education for 3 to 5 year-olds. It is sometimes operated as part of a primary school.
NVQ	A National Vocational Qualification is a qualification that is awarded for competent performance in work-based activities.
Office for Standards in Education	OFSTED is the government department responsible for the inspection and regulation of childcare, schools, colleges, children's services, teacher training and youth work. Website: www.OFSTED.gov.uk
OFSTED	*See* Office for Standards in Education.
OTT	Overseas Trained Teacher.
P1 to P7	In Scotland, primary year groups are referred to as P1 for the first year at school, when pupils are 5 years old, up to P7 for the last year, at age 11.
PANDA	Performance and Assessment Reports are produced by OFSTED. They include information about the context of the school, standards and value-added measures. Website: www.standards.dfes.gov.uk/locate/management/educationbodies/panda or https://www.epanda.rmplc.co.uk
PE	Physical Education.
PGCE	*See* Postgraduate Certificate of Education.
PMLD	Profound and Multiple Learning Difficulties.
Postgraduate Certificate of Education	A PGCE is usually achieved after studying for one year, post degree. Open to holders of ordinary or honours degrees.
Primary School	Primary schools are open to pupils between 5 and 11 years old. They may include classes for Nursery (3 to 5 year-olds), Reception (4 and 5 year-olds), Infants (5 to 7 year-olds) and Juniors (7 to 11 year-olds).

Private School	Also known as an independent school or public school. It is run outside the local education authorities. It does not have to deliver the National Curriculum, although many do. It receives no funds from the state, being funded by fees paid by parents of pupils. Website: www.isc.co.uk
PRU	*See* Pupil Referral Unit
PSHE	Personal Social and Health Education.
PSLD	Physical and Severe Learning Difficulties.
Public School	Although called a public school it is in fact a private school. It is also known as an independent school. *See* Private School.
Pupil Referral Unit	A PRU is a school for pupils who have been excluded from school.
QCA	*See* Qualifications and Curriculum Authority.
QTS	Teachers must have achieved Qualified Teacher Status to be eligible to work in schools in England and Wales. It is achieved on passing an appropriate teaching qualification such as a B.Ed or PGCE, and successfully completing one year of teaching.
Qualification, Curriculum and Assessment Authority for Wales	Now merged with the Welsh Assembly Government's Department for Education Lifelong Learning and Skills (DELLS). Website: www.accac.org.uk
Qualifications and Curriculum Authority	The QCA regulates external qualifications and provides advice on the school curriculum, pupil assessment and qualifications for the state sector in England. Website: www.QCA.org.uk
RC	Roman Catholic.
RE	Religious Education. Also see RS.
Reception	Reception classes, the first class in infant schools, are for 4 and 5 year-olds.
RS	Religious Studies.
S1 to S6	In Scotland, year groups are referred to as S1 for the first year at secondary school up to S6 for the last year at school.
SATs	*See* Standard Assessment Tests.
School Holidays	Most schools usually have two weeks holiday at Christmas, two weeks holiday at Easter, six weeks holiday in the summer and one week's holiday in the middle of each term. The actual dates may vary slightly between regions.
Scottish Executive Education Department	SEED is responsible for administering policy on pre-school and school education, children and young people, tourism, culture and sport in Scotland. Website: www.scotland.gov.uk
Scottish Executive Enterprise, Transport and Lifelong Learning Department	ETLLD works to support business, encourage enterprise, improve skills and employability and develop an efficient transport and communications infrastructure. Its remit includes further and higher education, and lifelong learning in Scotland. Website: www.scotland.gov.uk/About/Departments/ETLLD
Scottish Qualifications Authority	SQA is the government body responsible for developing, maintaining and certificating national qualifications in schools and further education in Scotland.
SEBD	Social, Emotional and Behavioural Difficulties.
Secondary School	Children attend secondary schools between the ages of 11 and 16, except in areas that have middle schools. Some secondary schools have sixth forms which are open to pupils aged 16 to 18.
SEED	*See* Scottish Executive Education Department.
Selective School	Any school that selects pupils on the basis of ability.
SEN	Special Educational Needs.
SENCO	Special Educational Needs Co-ordinator.

Sixth Form	Some schools offer pupils the opportunity to stay at school to continue their studies after they have completed their GCSEs (usually at age 16). There are also sixth-form colleges where pupils can study for GCE A Levels or re-sit GCSEs.
SLD	Severe Learning Difficulties.
SMT	A school's Senior Management Team usually includes the Headmaster, Deputy Head, Assistant Head, Bursar.
Special School	These schools cater for pupils with significant physical, emotional or behavioural issues. Not to be confused with specialist schools. *See* below.
Specialist School	State secondary schools that specialise in a specific area such as languages, sport, technology or art.
SQA	*See* Scottish Qualifications Authority.
Standard Assessment Tests	SATs are national tests taken by all pupils at the end of Key Stage 1 (aged 7), Key Stage 2 (aged 11) and Key Stage 3 (aged 14), in English, Mathematics and Science.
Standard Grade Examinations	The examinations taken by pupils in Scotland at the end of compulsory education.
State School	A school that is government funded, run within the local education authority, open to all pupils, with no selection process and no fees paid by parents.
TA	*See* Classroom Assistant.
TDA	*See* Training and Development Agency.
Term Time	Pupils attend school for 195 days each year. In England and Wales the autumn term runs from September to December, the spring term from January to March, and the summer term from April to July. Each term there is one week half-term holiday. In Scotland, the autumn term runs from August to December, the spring term from January to March/April and the summer term from April to June/July.
Training and Development Agency	The aim of the TDA (previously TTA) is to support the raising of standards in schools by improving the training and development of the school workforce. Website: www.tda.gov.uk
TTA	Teacher Training Agency, now known as the Training and Development Agency, *see* above.
Upper School	In some areas, pupils leave their primary schools at 8 or 9 to study at a middle school, before going on to an upper school aged 12 or 13.
VA	*See* Voluntary Aided School.
VI	Visually impaired.
Voluntary Aided School	A VA school is mainly funded by its local education authority. The buildings are usually owned by a charitable foundation. The governing body employs the staff, sets the admission criteria and contributes to building and maintenance costs.
Voluntary Controlled School	This type of school is run by the local education authority. It employs the school's staff, and runs the admission procedure. The school's land and buildings are normally owned by a charity, which appoints some of the members of the governing body.
Year Group	In England and Wales the primary and secondary school system is divided into year groups, from Year 1 for 5 year-olds to Year 11 for 16 year-olds.